PROFIT
FROM THE
CORE

PROFIT
FROM THE
CORE

A Return to Growth in
Turbulent Times

———

CHRIS ZOOK WITH JAMES ALLEN

Harvard Business Press
Boston, Massachusetts

Printed in the United States of America
14 13 12 11 10   5 4 3 2

Library of Congress Cataloging-in-Publication Data

Zook, Chris, 1951–
    Profit from the core : a return to growth in turbulent times / Chris Zook ; with James Allen.
        p. cm.
    Rev. ed. of: Profit from the core : growth strategy in an era of turbulence. 2001.
    Includes bibliographical references and index.
    ISBN 978-1-4221-3111-4 (hbk. : alk. paper)   1. Corporations—Growth.
2. Industrial management.   3. Corporate profits.   I. Allen, James, 1960–
II. Title.
    HD2746.Z66 2010
    658.15'5—dc22
                                                                    2009048038

The paper used in this publication meets the requirements of the American National Standard for Permanence of Paper for Publications and Documents in Libraries and Archives Z39.48-1992.

Contents

Preface

The global financial crisis and the rough road to recovery have brought the power of a company's core business back into sharp focus. Like a collective commercial death wish, global market values rose in 2007 by a staggering 20 percent (denominated in dollars), reaching $61 trillion by year end. In just five years, $38 trillion had apparently been created in the stock markets—more value in terms of market capitalization than the global stock markets had recorded in their entire history.

But where did it really come from? In some cases, as we have found, not the right places. Crises of the core have appeared everywhere. AIG, the poster child of the financial collapse, described its error as getting too far away from its "core" of insurance products by falling in love with the seductive interloper of complex, hedged securities. When Citibank combined with Travelers insurance it was heralded by its CEO Sandy Weill as the "model financial institution of the future." Yet, here was Citi in 2009, plummeting close to zero valuation, having created no economic value (precrisis).

These "crises of the core" have been epidemic, and not only in financial services. The bankruptcy of General Motors in June 2009 was foreshadowed by its remarkable loss of market share, from 44 percent in 1983 to just 22 percent in 2009, in its core U.S. light-vehicle market. Yet, over these decades GM was investing to enter businesses ranging from robotics to IT consulting (EDS) while its rival, Toyota, was waging mechanized warfare on the core of GM in the United States. Or consider Eastman Kodak, the company that in 1996 ruled the roost in photography. Kodak has seen its share price plummet since that time by 97 percent, with a market capitalization level in early 2009 of only about $700 million for this iconic core business.

During a single week in 2008, the global indexes declined by $8 trillion, as much as in the first eighteen months of the Internet bubble burst. In fact, we have seen this picture—or something resembling it—once before. In 1999, fueled by investor hyperbole, the value of stocks on all global exchanges blew away the previous world record for expansion. During that year, the total value of all traded stocks increased by $10 trillion, a staggering sum at the time, driving the global valuation to $35 trillion.

It was in these heady days, at the height of the Internet bubble, that *Profit from the Core* was first published in 2001. When the bubble collapsed, $12 trillion of market value quickly evaporated into the ether. "Focus on your core" became a watchword of the day, and this book was embraced by many management teams, who used it as a Rorschach test to ask themselves whether they had strayed too far into cyberspace, and, just perhaps, had lost sight of their real strength—their real core. Even Intel, one of the world's most focused and sophisticated companies, was struggling to overcome a crisis of the core, having redirected massive cash flow and attention into more than 150 new dot-com-related investments and allowing defeated, historic competitors like Advanced Micro Devices back into the game. Andy Grove, former CEO of Intel, recommended this book for reading by his management team, and the ideas about strategic focus in *Profit from the Core* became a centerpiece in their internal debates about strategy.

Profit from the Core was a paean to industrial sobriety in an era of "anything goes." It chronicled a litany of examples in which companies lost sight of what they were really good at, moved away from their strengths, and let their real competitive advantage erode in the process.

Our analysis and case examples showed that most companies with truly sustainable performance shared an extraordinary focus on a core, leadership economics to reinvest in the core, a uniquely loyal core customer base, and a well-defined repeatable model to extend the core.

Over the last few years, as the downturn loomed, we began to encounter more and more companies wondering whether they needed to return to focus on their core. That shared concern accelerated dramatically as management teams recognized the need for a more focused platform to use as a foundation for growth coming out of the financial crisis. The answer for most companies lies in a renewed focus on the core. Consider the following results of our analysis:

- During downturns, "weak cores" (followers) are the shock absorbers of the system, revealing margin swings that are two to five times that of the leader—a hidden liability of nurturing too many weak cores. That presents companies with strong, focused cores with an opportunity to take advantage of these weaknesses.

- Since the financial crisis started, we estimate that followers in a market have seen their values decline by nearly twice as much as leaders—presenting leaders with acquisition opportunities.

- About half of all of the profit in the world during 2007 came from six major industries—*all of which* are undergoing fundamental changes in their core business models above and beyond normal business investment. In a world of much lower profits, especially for weak core businesses, the future belongs to the smart leaders investing in their cores.

Against this background of once-in-a-generation challenges and opportunities, the idea of a revised edition of *Profit from the Core* took shape. The principles and findings of the book seem even more relevant given the structural crisis in business that the world is now facing:

- Sustained and profitable growth requires a strong, well-defined core.

- Most sustained profitable growth companies have leadership positions in their cores that form the epicenters of their strategies.

- The number-one rule of strategy is to discourage your competitors from investing in your core.

- The greatest source of strategic error, we find, stems from an inaccurate understanding of the core and its full potential.

- Strong cores often contain hidden assets that prove to be the seeds of the next wave of growth—the topic of my most recent book, *Unstoppable*.[1]

- The key to sustained and profitable growth is to find a repeatable formula that utilizes the most powerful and differentiated strengths in your core and applies them to a series of new "adjacent" markets.

To make this revised edition of *Profit from the Core* a useful guide to the search for sustainable growth, we have updated the key examples, added new ones, and rendered the lessons learned in a way that management teams can use as a tool to reflect on the way forward in today's economy. Turbulent conditions create confusion, blurred boundaries, less time to react, less tolerance for error, and often fewer resources. Yet they also create unique opportunities to strengthen and expand strong cores, and even to invest to reshape the structure of your industry ahead of competitors.

We hope you enjoy the book and prosper from its ideas.

Acknowledgments

Our first debt of gratitude is to the clients of Bain & Company, who allow us to participate on a daily basis with them on the front lines of some of the most dynamic and challenging business battle-grounds. It is to these smart and hardworking executives, some in seemingly impossible jobs, that we dedicate this book.

We also thank our partners at Bain & Company. Although we did the writing of the book on our own time, the data, client contacts, anecdotes, and support infrastructure are all Bain. Our first version of this acknowledgment, which included the name of each person who contributed an anecdote, advice, or an idea, listed more than eighty individuals, so we abandoned the idea of the itemized list, opting instead for this single heartfelt and deep thank you.

We especially are grateful to Tom Tierney, former managing director at Bain, who encouraged our writing of this book from the beginning. Steve Schaubert, our mentor and a senior Bain director, was one of the first to suggest this project and has been our most constant muse. Steve read every draft, generously leaving thoughtful and extensive voice mail messages the next day in response. Darrell Rigby has been a copilot through the entire project. He urged us to consider writing a book. Darrell has contributed ideas, material, contacts, wisdom, and friendship throughout.

Current and past partners of Bain Capital, especially Mitt Romney and Steve Pagliuca, were generous in sharing their experiences and making available to us case studies from their investment experiences.

I would also like to thank Phebo Wibbens, a brilliant consultant in Amsterdam, for assisting me in updating the key data in this revision. Marci Taylor returned to help me update the key examples, as she has done with every other book of mine. She added insight, accuracy, and inspiration whenever needed. Maggie Locher and Paul Judge were masterful in driving the editorial process and helping it all come together smoothly at the end. I have been consistently blessed with amazing people to work with at Bain, without whom this would not have been possible.

In addition, we have been blessed with excellent research assistants for support on specific pieces of work throughout. Tanya Lipiainen responded patiently whenever we requested "one more analysis." Murthy Nukala and Aditya Joshi were the first research associates to help with some of the original analyses that spurred this project forward.

Brenda Davis typed much of the manuscript, made editorial suggestions, provided psychological counseling, and has been the perfect assistant in every way.

Our editors at the Harvard Business School Press, Melinda Adams Merino, Barbara Roth, Sylvia Weedman, and Marjorie Williams, have provided inspiration when it mattered and have patiently nursed us through our first attempt to write a book. Thank you. In addition, we thank Walter Kiechel for urging us to write a book on growth several years ago, when he first saw our early Bain presentation.

We especially wish to thank Donna, Chris's wife, who allowed her dining room table to become "ground zero" for the most intense writing phase, which also displaced our wonderful families in some way on a regular basis.

Finally, Chris thanks his father, Nicholas Zook, a newspaperman and writer, for patiently trying to teach his son to write—perhaps the toughest task of all.

1

Desperately Seeking Growth

In a world of turbulent economies and scarce resources, are you wondering where your next wave of profitable growth will come from? Perhaps your industry is changing in a way that makes you wonder whether it might be time to redefine the business model that has been so productive for so many years. Or maybe your resources are spread too thin and you are fighting competitors on too many global fronts. Perhaps you suspect that your core business still has untapped profit growth potential, but you are not sure where it is.

If you can see your company in any of these situations, the findings of this book may surprise and interest you. The most important issue faced by all management teams is how to grow their companies profitably over the long term. Today, the odds for winning the long-term growth game are worse than ever. Many management teams need to reconsider and even rediscover their real core. Consider how the goal posts have moved for management:

- Investors are giving management teams less time than ever to prove themselves. For instance, shareholders are shifting in and out of stocks at five times the rate they did a few decades ago, demanding not merely growth, but growth each and every quarter.

- Even in the best of times, our analysis shows that nine out of ten management teams fail to grow their companies profitably. Given investor expectations of quarter-by-quarter growth, ninety-nine out of one hundred management teams will fail to meet shareholder expectations.

- Shareholders tolerate failure less than ever before. Between 1999 and 2006, the average tenure of departing CEOs in the United States declined from ten years to just over eight. One study of departing CEOs in America found that the 40 percent with the shortest tenure had lasted an average of fewer than two years. The lower half of this group had stayed on the job for only eight months.

The rules of the game are continually changing. As we demonstrate later in this book, turbulence in industries has increased by a factor of more than three over the past few decades. An unprecedented two-thirds of businesses and more than 50 percent of profits (reinvestment funds) in the world are in turbulent industries such as telecommunications, media, newspapers, airlines, and automobiles.

It is no wonder, then, that participants in a game that's impossible to play, much less win, are now particularly receptive to the soothing, dulcimer tones of pundits who suggest deceptively simple (and consistently incorrect) strategies for winning an extremely complex, multifaceted game. Their siren song seduces with its revolutionary appeal: "Discard the old, leave your historic core business behind, and set out for the promised land." Sometimes this advice leads to the right course. Yet, as we argue in this book and demonstrate with examples and extensive empirical data, it usually *does not* solve the fundamental problem and can even aggravate the underlying cause of inadequate profitable growth. Like the ancient mariners of the *Iliad*, those managers who respond to the siren song of growth can experience brief periods of euphoria. But when they finally awaken to reality, they often find themselves heading straight for the shoals.

Moreover, during and following the world economic crisis that started in 2007, the weaker businesses are proving to be the "shock absorbers" of the system. These businesses face far greater swings in margin and drops in valuation than the leaders, and they risk losing it all. During such times, it is especially incumbent on each management team to understand its core and remember that in strategy and the application of force in business, it is the choice and depth of focus—and not the breadth and speed of expansion—that lead to sustained, profitable growth.

We have found that the key to unlocking hidden sources of growth and profits is usually not to abandon the core business but to focus on it with renewed vigor and a new level of creativity. We have also found that often the most successful businesses are at greatest risk of succumbing to the siren song. Ironically, our research shows that the management teams running the strongest core businesses are the ones who most consistently underestimate their full economic potential. Consider the following examples of four companies that moved away from a core business in search of greener pastures.

Case 1: Bausch & Lomb

Bausch & Lomb got started in the ophthalmic business in 1853, when German immigrant Jacob Bausch opened a small store in Rochester, New York, to sell European optical imports. Over the next 120 years, the business developed slowly and carefully, step by step, just like the work of the meticulous eye doctors whom it served. By 1973, Bausch & Lomb had grown to $235 million in sales and was the leader in its instrument and lens businesses.

Then everything changed. In the mid-1970s, Bausch & Lomb obtained from an independent Czechoslovakian scientist the patents for *spin casting*, a process for making soft contact lenses. Spin casting not only produced lenses that were more comfortable than those on the market but did so at a lower cost. At the time, the standard procedure for creating a lens was to lathe it from a button of hard plastic. With spin casting, a drop of polymer is spun in a shaped dish and then stabilized under ultraviolet light to make the lens. The lenses created are "soft" because the liquid polymer sets in a form that is softer and more flexible than that of the hard plastic used in lathing. These more flexible lenses have proven to be better for the health of the eye and are easier for the optometrist to fit. They have also allowed for greater productivity throughout the value chain, from manufacturer to end user.

The soft contact lens was one of those breakthroughs that crack open and transform the competitive dynamics and market size in an industry. Throughout the mid-1980s, Bausch & Lomb developed and executed brilliant strategy, driving one competitor after another out of the market and causing others, locked into high-cost lathing methods, to disinvest in the business. The company's share of new lens fittings rose to 40 percent of the market, several times larger than that of its nearest competitors, American Hydron and Coopervision. Bausch & Lomb continued to invest in the business, buying the leading manufacturer of gas-permeable lenses, Polymer Technologies, to round out its product line. The company became a darling of Wall Street, outperforming the market over this period by more than 200 percent, with high, growing, and consistent earnings reports.

Then, as competitors began attacking its position with new technologies such as cast molding (also a low-cost method), Bausch & Lomb began to divert its attention from its core business, spending the cash flow from its lens and solutions businesses in new areas. "The core business is eroding, margins will erode as competitors enter . . . Use the cash to find new sources of growth," sang the sirens. The management team invested in products sold by other health professionals, such as electric toothbrushes, skin ointments, and hearing aids, but they established no obvious linkage between these products and the core lens business.

Slowly but surely, with resources and management attention distracted, Bausch & Lomb's contact lens business flattened out. The stock that had risen from $3 per share in 1973 to $56 per share in 1991 plummeted to less than $33 per share in 2003. Moreover, Johnson & Johnson entered the contact lens business by heavily funding a new acquisition, Vistakon, with a new product idea: disposable lenses. Of course, disposable lenses are not much different from regular lenses, except that they are sold at a lower price in packages of twelve or twenty-four. What better company to have introduced this product than the one-time cost and technology leader, Bausch & Lomb? Instead, Bausch & Lomb's market share declined to 16 percent, which put the company in third place behind Johnson & Johnson and Ciba Vision.

With its core strength squandered, Bausch & Lomb never really rebounded. In 2006, the company recalled one of its key eye-care products. The following year, Bausch & Lomb faced 344 product liability claims. Sales were again slipping, leading one analyst at J.P. Morgan to comment: "Returns across all of Bausch & Lomb's businesses are poor and notably behind competitor averages." By May 2007, when Warburg Pincus agreed to purchase the company for $4.5 billion, Bausch & Lomb was completely focused on eye care again, but it was now up against well-funded competitors like Alcon, Johnson & Johnson, and Novartis. If the company had not lost its focus on the core, it probably would not have turned out this way.[1]

Case 2: Amazon.com

Amazon.com began as the poster child of the Internet economy, and ended up as one of the few lasting success stories of that era. Most of the dot-com businesses that began during the heady years of the Internet bubble have not survived. But a few, such as eBay and Amazon.com, have successfully navigated the dual challenge of retaining focus even as they faced pressure to constantly adapt and redefine their core.

Amazon.com got its start in 1995 with the online selling of a product with a notoriously inefficient, multitier distribution channel: books. The typical offline bookstore returns more than

40 percent of the books that appear on its shelves for credit. The reasons returns are so high are that it is impossible for bookstores to predict which titles will become bestsellers and that a large number of "standard" books must be stocked in inefficient lots of two or three. The Amazon model bypasses this inefficiency by centralizing distribution and by getting its money from the consumer up front, often before the publisher needs to be paid. Moreover, Jeff Bezos, Amazon's founder and CEO, recognized that Amazon had the potential to be more than just a low-cost channel for book purchasing. With the introduction of book reviews written by customers, Amazon made itself a community website through which consumers could voice their views about the books they were purchasing. Based on the power of this business model, market capitalization rose to more than $30 billion in 1999 on $500 million of sales. During this period, Amazon raised the stakes, trying to become what Bezos calls "a place where you can buy anything and everything."

Suddenly, Amazon no longer confined itself to targeting the inefficient, multistep value chain of the bookseller (and, somewhat later, the video store); it began to compete with Wal-Mart and The Home Depot. Amazon moved with lightning speed into power tools, consumer electronics, garden furniture, and even cosmetics. By 2000 cumulative losses had mounted to $1.2 billion, and investor nervousness was high, reflected in a 70 percent stock price decline.

But, unlike Bausch & Lomb, Amazon parlayed this period of turbulence into a view of its "core of the core" that was even more compelling than the product itself. Its unique online software—the commercial engine of the company—proved much more fundamental than a new model for selling books. In 2008, the company hit $19.2 billion in revenue, with a 23 percent return on invested capital. Though media (books, movies, music) still remain a highly profitable 58 percent of revenues, other areas have grown. Yet a closer look reveals that 30 percent of Amazon's total sales come from its third-party seller business.

Amazon's journey has led it to a strong and stable core, despite the dangers it has had to navigate along the way. In Jeff Bezos's words: "It helps to base your strategy on things that won't change . . . I very rarely get asked, 'What's not going to change in the next five to ten years?' At Amazon.com we're always trying to figure that out."[2]

Case 3: Cooke Optics

Cooke Optics was founded in England in 1890 for the purpose of creating the highest-quality lenses for still photography, a new and fast-growing market at the time. Cooke quickly became the gold standard in the industry, and the camera taken to the South Pole in 1907 by explorer Sir Ernest Shackleton and his crew was fitted with a Cooke lens. During World War I, Cooke lenses were critical for high-resolution aerial photography. The advent of silent films put Cooke lenses on the front of many cameras in leading movie studios. As the small company evolved, it expanded into specialized zoom lenses and even higher-quality "prime" nonzoom lenses. In 1946, Cooke was sold to the Rank Group, a company with no related holdings or interest in preserving Cooke's quality image. Over the next few decades, Rank moved into postproduction studios, resorts, and casinos, leaving Cooke at the end of the line when it came to getting attention from management or resources for investment. Cooke stagnated. Comparing this state of affairs with the company's proud history, a thirty-seven-year employee lamented, "The place was so run down that sea-gull feathers would float down through the holes in the roof."[3] The company was finally rescued in 1998 by Les Zellan, a theater-lighting specialist who had kept an eye on Cooke for decades, watching its once-valuable core business erode. In 1998, he got his chance and took it, buying Cooke for only $3 million. Since then, the core lens business, neglected for nearly five decades, has been brought back to life with a new lens that has superior focusing technology. The lens caught on almost immediately and has been used for shooting such hit films as *Hairspray*, three of the Harry Potter movies (*Prisoner of Azkaban*,

Goblet of Fire, and *Half-Blood Prince*), and *The Bourne Supremacy* and such television series as *Bones* and *Grey's Anatomy*. The company's continued success and growth show the potential to profit from and renew a once-strong core.

Case 4: The Gartner Group

The Gartner Group was founded in 1979 by Gideon Gartner, a stock analyst at the securities trading firm of Oppenheimer who specialized in tracking IBM and its few competitors in those days. The original purpose of the Gartner Group was to sell information about IBM to investment bankers and stockbrokers. Shortly after the founding of the company, its focus was broadened to include customers deciding on equipment to buy or starting negotiations with IBM for hardware. In the burgeoning market for business computers, consumer need proved to be large, and Gartner focused entirely on becoming, in a sense, a consumer clearinghouse for customer data and expert opinion on products.

Saatchi & Saatchi purchased the company in the mid-1980s as part of its attempt to unify consulting and advertising services in a single company—a misconceived growth strategy in itself that soon imploded. Saatchi became disillusioned with the consulting business in 1989 and sold Gartner to Bain Capital, a private equity firm specializing in buying noncore or undermanaged corporate assets.

For $60 million, Bain Capital purchased a company that was growing at about 15 percent annually, had reached $55 million in revenues, and had margins of only about 10 percent, a disappointment to its former parent. But Bain Capital saw something more in the Gartner Group than a small, low-margin consultancy. The more Bain managers studied the company's core business, the more they began to believe that Gartner would have a much greater opportunity for growth and for margin expansion if they looked at it not as a consulting business but as a vehicle for collecting, packaging, and distributing high-value syndicated data.

Under the ownership of Bain Capital, Gartner refocused on becoming a consumer clearinghouse for customer responses and an honest broker of advice on hardware and software purchases. Gartner's growing company subscriber base gave it proprietary access to thousands of companies whose managers were willing to comment for the record on their experiences with buying and installing computer systems. No longer did a corporate management information system department need to commission expensive outside consulting studies for the purpose of obtaining objective data; it could rely on Gartner studies, which were less costly and more timely than its own. Gartner built strong barriers to imitation through its subscriber base and its database of benchmarks that allowed it to expand its margins from about 10 percent to 30 percent.

Bain Capital had a three-part growth strategy for Gartner:

1. Turn Gartner into a syndicated data and research company with a much more scalable model than consulting.

2. Expand geographically beyond its high East Coast customer concentration into the West and Europe by adding salespeople.

3. Deepen the product line in the most leveraged, vertical, industry-focused application markets.

The suggested strategy of looking at the original core business in a new way was successful. The company grew from $55 million in 1980 to $295 million in 1995 under Bain Capital's ownership to $734 million in 1999 as a public company. Over this period, Gartner solidified its hold in its core business. Bain Capital sold the company to Dun & Bradstreet for approximately a twenty times return on its equity, and Dun & Bradstreet subsequently sold Gartner in an initial public offering at an additional twenty times multiple. Ten years later, in 2008, Gartner continued its momentum, achieving 40 percent share of the IT research market (four times the size of its nearest competitor), $1.3 billion in revenues, and $213 million in earnings before interest and tax—growing at a healthy 12 percent through the period.

What is notable about this growth story, other than the four hundred times return on equity invested, is the fact that the new owners had a different take on the core business, seeing it as a syndicated data and research enterprise rather than a consultancy. The ability to creatively see the core in a new light and act on it is a theme that we will return to throughout this book.

Our Mission

In each of the above cases, and hundreds of others that we have examined, we see a tendency for strong core businesses to lose momentum by virtue of premature abandonment, miscalculation, or overreaching in search of new growth. Our intention in this book is not to suggest that we have a one-size-fits-all solution for problems with growth. Rather, our intention is to suggest that many of the common cures prescribed in the popular business literature need to be balanced against the weight of evidence on real company experiences. What we offer is a set of practical and proven principles, diagnostic tests, and questions for management teams to use as tools for reexamining or revising their strategies in search of the next wave of profitable growth. In our quest to understand the dynamics of growth, we drew on the following fact base:

- About two hundred case studies in Bain & Company and in the public record

- Interviews and discussions with about one hundred senior executives

- A database of 1,854 public companies in seven countries followed for more than ten years

- Numerous pieces of focused empirical analysis concerning sources of profitable growth

- The records of many private equity firms—including Bain Capital, which generously shared many of its case studies with us

- Extensive examination of the existing literature (cited throughout the book) and of secondary data

The lack of empirical data behind many business "cure-alls" has prompted one Oxford don to proclaim management science a "phony academic subject, a shallow contemporary shibboleth promoting a noxious cant."[4] We are not that cynical. We consider management science to be highly productive, but we also understand that it is in its infancy. More important, we maintain that there do exist a few lasting principles of business strategy that have clearly driven results year after year, that apply across a wide range of industries, and that explain the results of both success and failure.

Defining Profitable Growth

We explored many definitions of profitable growth and settled on one that involves several dimensions. Throughout this book, we define *sustained growth* as growth in both revenues and profits over an extended period of time while total shareholder returns (share price and dividend reinvestment) exceed the cost of capital. Empirically, few companies in the long term create shareholder value without earning their cost of capital.

When we looked at the data, we identified targets that were at or below most of the strategic planning targets we found in a survey of strategic plans. These targets are (1) achieving 5.5 percent real (inflation-adjusted) growth in revenues and earnings and (2) earning one's cost of capital over an average of ten years. We examined the data company by company to control for accounting anomalies and one-time charges. The results of our screen are depicted in figure 1-1, showing the percentages of our full sample of companies that meet our revenue criterion, income criterion, and shareholder value creation criterion. Even with these relatively conservative and modest targets, we found that only about one company in eight, or

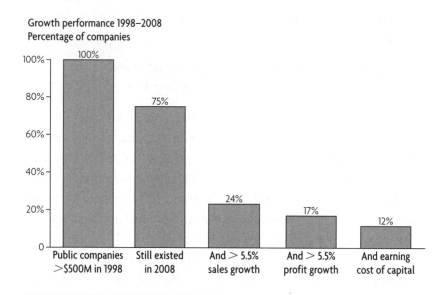

Growth performance 1998–2008
Percentage of companies

1-1 Few Companies Achieve Sustainable Growth Strategies

Source: Worldscope database; Bain analysis.

Note: Earning cost of capital defined as above average total shareholder return. 5.5% required growth rate is in *real terms* (i.e., after correction for inflation). Analysis of 2,000+ companies in 12 developed and emerging economies.

12 percent, or about one in ten companies, achieved sustained and profitable growth (or could be classified as a sustained value creator) over a decade that many would rank as among the best for the world economy. In contrast, our internal sample of targets from strategic plans showed that more than 90 percent of the companies examined had aimed at returns well in excess of these levels.

When we tightened the criteria a bit more, requiring 8 percent real growth (about 11 percent to 12 percent nominal currency growth in most of our major countries in this period), the percentage of sustained value creators declined to only 9 percent. In a survey of strategic plans, we found that the target of more than two-thirds of the businesses examined was at least at these levels. Yet the reality is that fewer than one in ten achieved it.

We found that companies that grew revenues but not profits did not create economic value in the long term (though they can create shareholder wealth in the short term in the stock market). Companies that grew profits but not revenues were on an unsustainable growth path that eventually petered out. Companies that grew both revenues and profits but did not earn their cost of capital eventually (recall that our period of analysis is ten years) lost their ability to find investors.[5] An extensive body of work on investor value creation supports this point of view.

Other measures of profitable growth that we considered are worth noting, along with their specific limitations. Stock price growth (adjusted for splits) is alluringly simple, but is dependent on the specific company's pay-out policy in dividends or share buybacks, which have, in the short term, only an indirect relation to operational or financial performance. Total enterprise market value growth is somewhat better. However, it is possible to grow total market value through mergers that neither help earnings nor create a sustained growth trajectory. Moreover, putting together several poorly performing companies to create a new one is not what our project was about.

Share of total industry profits or share of total industry value is an interesting measure of relative competitive success. However, it does not take into account absolute levels of growth or profitability, which could be declining. Moreover, it begs the question of the business boundaries, of what to include or exclude.

High total shareholder return is critical to sustained, profitable growth. Yet a company that did not grow, had no assets, and had positive cash flow would have infinite returns. Looking at returns in the absence of growth is as limiting in the context of our study as looking at growth in the absence of returns.

Finally, there are more specialized or exotic measures of profitable growth. One such measure is profit or value creation per employee. But this is at least as much a function of labor and capital intensity of the business as it is of sustained, profitable growth. A derivative measure of this is growth in value per employee. This, however, could be as much a function of shifting to more capital intensity as it is of performance and growth. These are interesting measures, but not what we were after.

Using the screen of earning the cost of capital in the long term and growing both revenues and profits worked well for us, though we urge management teams to supplement this metric with others, both short term and long term, in considering their own growth pattern.

Defining the Core

It is our thesis in this book that the foundation of sustained, profitable growth is a clear definition of a company's core business. A business can be defined from two related perspectives. The first (outside-in) is from the point of view of the outside world, with natural business boundaries defined by underlying market economics. The second (inside-out) is from the point of view of those inside the company, with the company's business boundaries defined by its unique core.

Here is an example of the distinction. Enterprise Rent-A-Car, Dollar Thrifty, and Avis are clearly in a business that external criteria define as car rental. The business involves purchasing and managing fleets, running automated reservation centers, managing a branch network, and serving customers who rent cars for various purposes. Within this business, however, the three companies have different cores. Enterprise is the market leader for insurance replacement and repair rentals. The company got its start in this distinct segment, building its suburban locations and business model to meet the needs of body shops and insurance companies. Dollar Thrifty's core business comes from leisure renters who don't mind having to pick up their rental cars and in conditions with minimal amenities. Avis's core is airport rentals. It sells heavily to corporate renters requiring speedy service, newer cars, a variety of business amenities, and, obviously, a network of prime airport locations. Each of these companies would view its core differently, and each would be right. Yet each participates in a rental car business that external economics is treating more and more as one competitive arena.

A different type of example is Gillette, which has had men's shaving products as its core business since its founding nearly one hundred years ago. After achieving a 70 percent market share in its core, Gillette sought growth in an unconventional way, looking beyond the limited shaving market. It redefined its core business more in terms of control and share of the checkout-counter displays at retail stores, leading it to expand into writing instruments, Duracell batteries, and other distribution-related products. The jury is out on the full success of this strategy. However, it is a case in which a company has redefined its core such that it no longer sits within the external boundaries marked on the map held by the rest of the business world.

To identify your core business, first identify the five following assets:

1. Your most potentially profitable franchise customers

2. Your most differentiated and strategic capabilities

3. Your most critical product offerings

4. Your most important channels

5. Any other critical strategic assets that contribute to the above (such as patents, brand name, position at a control point in a network)

When we begin a consulting assignment at Bain, we almost always ask first: "What is the business definition of where you compete?" "What is your core business and source of potential competitive advantage?" The answers to these questions require an understanding of each of the five dimensions.

A *Wall Street Journal* article in a past downturn announced "Corporate America Confronts the Meaning of a 'Core' Business." The article went on to recognize the complexity inherent in this task, noting: "Focus is in these days, both on Wall Street and in boardrooms across America, and this raises a surprisingly complex question: What constitutes a core business? Is it a product? A cache of intellectual property? A process? Or, is it a business design . . . that can be deployed across multiple industries?"[6] That complexity has only increased over time.

For some companies, the definition of the core business is not overly difficult; for others, it is extremely vexing. For all, it is important to have the clearest definition possible. In the case of Gillette, the core business would appear to be men's shaving products. This part of Gillette's business was its fastest-growing and most profitable component in 1910, and it remains so today. The key assets that constitute this core include some deep areas of competence such as expertise in the manufacturing of high-precision miniature items, proficiency in blade-sharpening and -handling technology, and skill in brand management. Gillette has used these assets to enter a variety of related businesses ranging from hair care products (Toni) to small electronic appliances (Braun) to toothbrushes (Oral-B) to batteries (Duracell). In some cases, as we discuss later in the book, these expansions were successful and drew on Gillette's core strength; in others, they proved unrelated distractions.

Companies such as Coca-Cola, UPS, Toyota, SAP, Nokia, Wal-Mart, and even Bain & Company have relatively well-defined cores that most executives can understand and use as platforms for profitable growth. In some companies, such as PepsiCo, there may be several different and distinct cores—in this case, the cola business and the salty snacks business of Frito-Lay.

For other companies such as AOL Time Warner, 3M, General Electric, or Siemens, however, the core business is much more difficult to define. These companies are the exception. Moreover, these types of highly complex or conglomerate-like companies less often appear in the ranks of sustained value creators.

Most conglomerates have not been able to manage multiple strong cores successfully. Conglomerates are underrepresented among our sustained value creators, consistent with the findings of many past studies on diversification. Moreover, we find that, overwhelmingly, the strongest performing multi-industrials, like Danaher or United Technologies Corp (UTC), exploit leadership positions in a few strong core businesses, which they drive into adjacent territory step by step, extending them to new customers, channels, products, or applications. Moreover, they often create value across these businesses with a relatively well-defined *repeatable formula* that is proved over and over and becomes central to the corporation in three ways:

- The way the company describes its strategy

- The way managers view the core of the company

- The way analysts perceive the company's distinct advantages and opportunities for growth

For the purposes of this book, we define the *core business* as that set of products, capabilities, customers, channels, and geographies that defines the essence of what the company is or aspires to be to achieve its growth mission—that is, to grow its revenue sustainably and profitably. We recognize that this is a loose definition that can lead to significant debate among management teams. There can be tension between what a company is and what it aspires to or needs to be for competitive reasons. And there is often a lack of proportion in the number of customers overall and the number of customers who really support profits—the classic 80/20 rule, which states that less than 20 percent of a customer base accounts for 80 percent of a company's profits. Inversely, this implies that most customers often do not define the core business; that is, they do not contribute to the growth mission. The essence of a company's growth strategy is to define the core business as we have defined it and to pour company resources into this core business until it achieves its full potential.

How to Approach This Book

In this book, we focus on a single theme: the extraordinary importance of creating a strong core business as a foundation for driving company growth.

We define the growth metrics that management should use precisely—the goal of management is to grow revenues and profits sustainably. Only this will create shareholder value over the long term. We define the core business as precisely as possible, emphasizing that the process of defining the core business is at the heart of what a management team must do and is inherently an imprecise science.

We fully acknowledge that the theme of seeking profit from the core is not new, and throughout the book we acknowledge extensive work done by others on this and related topics. We feel compelled to return to the theme for three reasons. First, the empirical data on the frequency with which management teams undervalue their core business is overwhelming. Why are their expectations so low? Second, focusing solely on a strong core business is necessary to but not sufficient for achieving sustainable growth. Management teams constantly meet with opportunities to move into related businesses, and at times such moves are absolutely necessary to strengthen the core and add new profit streams. How should management teams respond to this basic tension in business—when to focus on the core, when to pursue adjacent opportunities? Third, a management team must sometimes choose to make a fundamental change in the essence of the company's core business if it is to create new and sustainable growth. This is especially the case in any industry experiencing turbulent times. How should managers think about this decision—which involves more risk than any other they will make—to change the core in the interest of protecting the core?

To address these questions, we have structured this book around the three basic issues management must face in seeking profit from the core:

1. Build market power and influence in the core business or in a segment of that business.

2. Having done that, expand into logical and reinforcing adjacencies around the core.

3. Shift or redefine the core in response to industry turbulence.

In chapter 2, we discuss how to define a core business and illustrate how to obtain the full potential from a core business. We introduce the first paradox of growth: *The better performing of your business units are likely to be those operating the furthest below their full potential.* We have found that when most management teams seek to revitalize the growth of a company, they focus on the underperforming business units. We argue that growth requires focusing instead on increasing the performance of the best businesses, no matter how well they are doing at present. The best business is in the best position to deliver better growth.

We begin by presenting evidence that a strong core is the key source of competitive advantage and then go on to define core business boundaries, means for differentiation through gaining market power and influence, and reasons why many of the best core businesses often are performing below their full growth potential and have a set of classic sources of "hidden value." In turbulent industry situations, however, the ability to define the boundaries of a core business becomes more challenged and the importance of traditional measures of market share, therefore, less relevant. In many traditional industries, competition among identical business models is the rule, yet more and more today we are observing competition among fundamentally different business models. Dealing with this increased competitive complexity is one of the primary issues facing business strategists in many industries.

In chapter 3, we shift to the topic of what we call *adjacency expansion*, moving into a set of new but related businesses around the core business. In discussing adjacency expansion, we introduce the second paradox of growth: *The stronger your core business, the more opportunities you have both to move into profitable adjacencies and to lose focus.* Chapter 3 examines the typical patterns exhibited by those companies with the best records of historical growth. Some businesses, such as Toyota, Tetra Pak, McDonald's, Intel, Cisco Systems, and UPS, have grown for decades, if not longer, by systematically expanding into logical business adjacencies around a relatively stable core. We reinforce the findings of dozens of studies with our own data showing how many of the most promising growth strategies were derailed by overexpansion or choice of the wrong adjacency. Industry turbulence, however, sometimes makes it necessary for managers to place more bets at the periphery of the business to hedge against uncertainties instead of marching forward on a planned path for growth, year after year, as seen in the expansion of stores in retail.

In chapter 4, we address when and how to redefine a core business, especially when faced with industry turbulence. Here we introduce the third paradox of growth: *The management teams that have been most successful in building a strong core business and that have benefited from adjacency expansion are also the most vulnerable to industry turbulence.* In some ways, this theme of redefinition runs *sotto voce* throughout every chapter of the book. The record of long-lived strong core businesses successfully redefining themselves and reasserting leadership is not an encouraging one for legacy companies.

Chapter 4 also examines the increasingly close linkage between organization and growth strategy. In these situations of turbulence and short response times, the popular epithet "structure follows strategy" is being rewritten as "sometimes structure *determines* strategy." The ability to react quickly and refine strategy based on marketplace events is a major source of competitive advantage for many successful companies.

In chapter 5, we provide some guidelines for the process of developing and refining growth strategy. We also conclude with the fourth paradox of growth: *All organizations inhibit growth.* In today's turbulent business environment, change—in company strategies, structures, and people—is crucial to achieving sustained profitable growth. To master change, managers must pursue it, not resist it.

While the message of profit from the core is simple, the challenges management faces in translating it into action are extraordinary. Each paradox of growth threatens to defeat management, to decrease the odds of achieving sustainable, profitable growth. The failure rate is as high as 99 percent.

We believe that the three elements of growth strategy listed above are as relevant to stable industries, such as food processing or textiles, in a long-term equilibrium as they are to turbulent industries, ranging from electric utilities to online retail, careening from disequilibrium to disequilibrium. However, in turbulent conditions many of the common strategic rules of thumb need to be adapted.

A great deal of excellent work has been done by academic researchers and business practitioners on the topic of how traditional rules of strategy, first developed for a stable, capital-intensive industry, now must be adapted for businesses facing the need to redefine themselves (especially information-intense businesses) around economic turbulence. For instance, Clayton Christensen has described brilliantly how new competitors can emerge and thrive using "disruptive" technologies, building power in low-profit marginal customers as the incumbent helplessly watches on.[7] Carl Shapiro has described how the peculiar economics of information businesses require a new set of economic rules to develop robust business strategies.[8] Others have examined why large companies are slow to adapt to change or why market share is less important than it used to be. Throughout the book we gratefully acknowledge and build on this foundational work.

We have referred repeatedly to the paradoxical aspects of growth strategy in business. Certainly, the world is full of paradoxes. To hit a golf ball farther, you hold the club more loosely. To right a car during an icy skid, you take your foot off the brake. To make a plant grow stronger and more quickly, you cut it back.

Overlying all of the analysis in this book is a final paradox: *From focus comes growth; by narrowing scope one creates expansion.* It is remarkable to us how, despite the array of growth opportunities presenting themselves to most management teams, the most reliable and consistent solution is to profit from the core.

2

The Profitable Core

The idea of a core set of economic activities is as old as management science itself. David Ricardo's writings in 1817 on comparative advantage in trade were, in part, an attempt to determine the core set of activities around which a nation should focus its resources. Alfred Marshall's work in the late 1800s on increasing returns to scale anticipates the idea of business definition and competitive advantage from a growing core. Economists in the 1930s and 1940s examining antitrust matters constantly encountered the issues of business definition and how far market power extended from a core business.

During the 1980s, an era of breakup artists and corporate restructuring, many business writers, such as Michael Porter, documented how corporations' returns declined as their activities became more diffused and their core became less well defined. The issue of strategic focus has been examined in writings ranging from the stick-to-your-knitting theme of *In Search of Excellence* to the work on core competence by Hamel and Prahalad to the idea of a central core vision in *Built to Last*.[1]

Profit from the Core builds on this by providing overwhelming evidence that shows how often a strong core coupled with focused leadership—the stronger and more focused, the better—is often at the epicenter of the most successful cases of sustained and profitable growth. By contrast, we find equally overwhelming evidence of how inadequate self-knowledge about the real potential of the core—or misjudgments about the extent to which perceived strengths can really be extended into new areas—leads to strategic difficulties. In the rest of this book we discuss how to define and strengthen a core, how to determine the best growth opportunities emanating out from a core, and when to step back and redefine the core.

The Power of Focusing on the Core

Companies that have very few highly focused core businesses account for most of the sustained growth companies. The historical record shows that most diversified companies should narrow and focus their activities to create fewer growth platforms, while companies with multiple mediocre business positions are better off restructuring their portfolios to develop, strengthen, and reinforce a single core if they can create one that possesses what we refer to as *leadership economics*. The evidence clearly supports this viewpoint:

- Most companies that sustain value creation possess only one or two strong cores.

- Private equity companies often achieve their greatest success by buying orphan businesses from diffuse conglomerates, thereby creating focus where there had been none before.

- Spin-offs usually create both focus and value.

- Diversification is associated with lower average valuations than are typical of companies with focused cores.

- Acquisitions made for the purpose of expanding scale in a core business have a success rate that is at least twice that of acquisitions to diversify and expand "scope."

- The few companies that became smaller and still created value—that "shrank to grow"—are those that restructured to focus on a strong core, often eventually to turbocharge their growth again.

Evidence from Sustained Value Creators

An examination of the companies that have sustained both value creation and at least 5.5 percent annual growth over ten years shows that nearly 80 percent of these sustained value creators had one core business with a leadership position in its "core of the core" (figure 2-1). These businesses were the source of most of their companies' profitable growth. Another 17 percent of sustained value creators had multiple cores around which they built their growth. We also looked at the difference between multi-core companies and single-core, more focused companies. Our findings show that conglomerates typically have a somewhat lower probability of attaining the sustained value creator threshold than single-core companies. However, there is a strong exception to this rule. Those conglomerates that

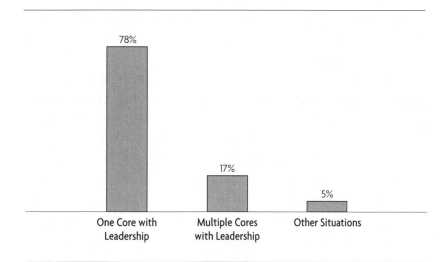

| 78% | | |
| One Core with Leadership | 17% Multiple Cores with Leadership | 5% Other Situations |

2-1 Sustained Value Creators Lead in Their Cores

Source: Worldscope database, OneSource, industry reports, Bain analysis.

Note: Core is defined as the business that creates a majority of the company's revenues. Leadership is defined as relative market share greater than 1.2.

have a large percentage of their portfolio in positions of leadership economics, and have a well-defined repeatable formula for adding value uniquely to businesses and new acquisitions (a differentiated management system), do outperform. Examples would be "themed" conglomerates like Procter & Gamble in consumer products, or purer conglomerates like Danaher and United Technologies. Each of these companies has a well-defined "way," a repeatable formula, that adds value from the center, at the corporate level. In fact, each company actually defines the description of its strategy around the elements of this repeatable formula such as the ACE program of United Technologies or the highly successful Danaher Business System.

Many of the sustained value creators that we examined followed a common pattern: a tightly focused, sustained value creating company pulls farther and farther ahead of its rival, which is embedded in a diversified company with no clear focus or core. For example, in soft drinks, PepsiCo (a food conglomerate until its recent breakup) trails Coca-Cola, a more focused competitor, in the soft drink business. Anheuser-Busch leads in the U.S. beer business, followed by Miller, which was part of a packaging foods conglomerate until combining with SAB. Motorola and Ericsson, both companies with many separate parts, follow Nokia in the cellular phone business. IBM and numerous other technology conglomerates follow EMC Corporation in data storage devices.

It is almost as if most growth strategies harbor a dark, destructive force that causes companies to reduce their focus on their core business and thereby to depart from the basis of their real differentiation. Consider the following questions: Why did Citibank acquire Travelers, an insurance company, in 1998 despite manifest opportunities and challenges in its banking core? Why did GM purchase Electronic Data Systems when it was under the greatest pressure in its core automotive business? Why did Vivendi pursue the noncore entertainment business so aggressively (and at great cost) when its core business was environmental services involving waste and water? Or, to return to an earlier example, why did Bausch & Lomb seemingly abandon its eye-care leadership to invest in hearing aids, ointments, and dental products—moves that collectively proved disastrous? These companies are run by smart people who must be familiar with the body of evidence proving the power of business focus and the need to outinvest competitors in their core business. So what happened?

Evidence from Private Equity

Impressive evidence of the strategic value of focusing on a strong core comes from companies that change their status from orphan businesses in large conglomerates to become freestanding businesses whose only cores are themselves. It is no wonder that private equity firms love to purchase noncore businesses from large conglomerates.

Consider the case of Accuride. Accuride sold truck rims and wheels to a concentrated number of original equipment manufacturer customers such as Ford, Volvo, General Motors, MAC, and Freightliner. Within Firestone Tire & Rubber Company, its previous owner, Accuride was an orphan. Its business was not even remotely related to any of Firestone's core tire or rubber businesses. Interestingly, it also competed against a number of other companies, such as Goodyear and Budd, for which the steel rim-and-wheel business was also secondary. Did the noncore nature of these businesses provide a growth opportunity for a company that might choose to invest and manage Accuride differently? Bain Capital thought so.

Upon acquisition by Bain Capital, Accuride's focus changed. The company was cut loose from the budget constraints, management neglect, and low status it had experienced at Firestone. As Mitt Romney, managing director of Bain Capital at the time (and subsequently a 2008 U.S. presidential candidate), observes, "It was now a case of grow or perish."[2] Accuride's executives studied the market and economics in a new way. They concluded that if they could get close to 100 percent market share of several major customers, they could tilt industry dynamics in their favor and capture the majority of the industry's pool of profits for the long term. This, in turn, could discourage Goodyear and Budd from investing heavily in what was by no means their core business. And, of course, competitor disinvestment is a desirable outcome for any strategy.

To achieve their goals, the Accuride executives added low-cost capacity and preemptively offered lower prices and superior terms that competitors could not quickly match. Romney continues, "Goodyear acted slowly and decided not to match. Masco was stunned and stopped investing in plant capacity. I can remember a winter day walking around its deserted, partially completed site with snow-covered equipment. Budd did open a Mexican facility. But by then it was over—game, set, and match."

Nowhere is the value of focus as clear as in a single-product company fighting for its life against less-focused competitors embedded in large conglomerates with many cross-cutting agendas and trade-offs. Accuride saw its market share relative to competitors go through the roof, its absolute share double, and its profitability rise 66 percent in less than two years. Bain Capital, for its insight into an undermanaged core business competing against other undermanaged core businesses, earned nearly twenty-five times return on its investment.

The power of focusing on the core proved a decisive factor in this success story. While there are few controlled experiments in business, because of the number of economic factors at play, there are many cases, such as Accuride, that demonstrate the power of reestablishing intense focus on a single core, building strength by acquiring competitors or by driving the profitable core through increased investment and a more aggressive strategy. Many of the most successful investments in the annals of leveraged buyouts and private equity firms stem from strategically undermanaged, noncore businesses (with profitable cores at their centers) that are purchased and revived by a new owner.

Evidence from Spin-offs

The experiences of companies that have split themselves up or spun off major divisions or groups as separate public companies offer still more evidence of the power of focus. David Sadtler, Andrew Campbell, and Richard Koch's examination of the aftermath of spin-offs found that they have led to an average 15 percent increase in the companies' relative competitive performance in the stock market.[3] In another study of more than one hundred companies that had undergone spin-offs, New York analyst Steven Bregman found that the spin-offs generated an annual rate of return from 1991 through 1996 of 37.2 percent, as compared to only a 17.5 percent increase in the Standard & Poor's index over the same period.[4]

PepsiCo provides an example of this positive spin-off effect. Over the past two decades, Coca-Cola has outperformed PepsiCo substantially, even though PepsiCo has performed well and provided total return to shareholders of 23 percent. Moreover, PepsiCo's fast-food restaurant business was lagging in its performance and falling behind that of another focused competitor, McDonald's. In 1997, PepsiCo spun off its $14 billion restaurant business, which consisted of Taco Bell, Kentucky Fried Chicken, and Pizza Hut.

Many who followed the company argued that the restaurant business was a drag on the beverage business and that the beverage businesses caused lack of focus on the noncore restaurants. One *Wall Street Journal* article even asserted that there was economic value destruction from the combination:

> Some analysts argue that Pepsi is a distant second to Coke in the profitable fountain business—selling syrup to restaurants for their soda fountains—precisely because of its ownership of fast-food chains. Coke's sales force can tell a restaurant that by offering Pepsi-Cola drinks it is putting money in the pockets of competitors Taco Bell and Pizza Hut.[5]

Management acknowledged to the investors that the restaurant business was diverting too much attention and time from its need to focus on the core. Former CEO Roger Enrico admitted that "a whole lot more focus would be very beneficial."[6]

At the time, one article called the restaurant business "an anchor pulling through the sand at the bottom of the ocean."[7] But since the spin-off, both the original core and the new restaurant business,

Yum! Brands, Inc. (the erstwhile Tricon Global Restaurants) have done well, the latter outperforming its reference group of restaurants by a factor of two.

Evidence from Diversification Studies

Further evidence of the power of a strong, singular core comes from studies of the impact of shareholder value on diversification (the opposite of focus on the core). One extensive empirical study was done by Constantinos Markides, who examined the extent and effects of corporate refocusing in the 1980s. Defining *refocusing* as a company's decision to reduce the scope of its activities in order to concentrate on the "core" business (that is, to reduce diversification), Markides found that more companies were refocusing in the 1980s than had done so in the 1960s. In the 1960s, only 1 percent of the top American companies were refocusing, while 25 percent were diversifying. In the 1980s, more than 20 percent of these companies were refocusing, while 8 percent were diversifying. In addition, his research showed that companies refocused by divesting unrelated businesses and acquiring related ones. Among the top one hundred U.S. companies from 1981 through 1987, more than 65 percent of acquisitions were related to the core business and nearly 58 percent of divestitures were unrelated to the core business. Markides also found that reducing diversification created market value, showing that a company's market value goes up nearly 2 percent on the day it announces its refocusing.[8]

Michael Porter, in a study published in the *Harvard Business Review* in 1987, also looked at the contribution of diversification to corporate performance. Analyzing the diversification histories of thirty-three large U.S. companies from 1950 through 1986, he found dismal track records. In fact, these corporations, on average, had divested more than half of their acquisitions in new industries and more than 60 percent of their acquisitions in entirely new fields. The average divestment rate in unrelated acquisitions was even higher—nearly 75 percent.[9]

A more recent Bain & Company study looked at 7,315 divestitures completed by 742 companies over the twenty-year period from 1987 through 2007. The study found that a set of companies identified as being the "best divestors" earned a return for shareholders that was 80 percent higher than the average company over that time. An example is the Swiss pharmaceutical company Roche. In 2000, the company sold off its flavors and fragrances, vitamins, and fine chemical businesses to focus investments more intensively on pharmaceuticals and related diagnostic products. Given that many of these businesses had been in the Roche portfolio for more than 50 years, this was not an easy decision. Yet, it was a necessary condition to make Roche the best-performing major pharmaceutical company in the world at the time.[10] More recently, David Harding and Sam Rovit have shown in their book *Mastering the Merger* that "scale deals" (acquisition of a company in the same business) perform significantly better than "scope deals" (acquisition of a company in a different business).[11] The average success rate (defined as creating economic value reflected in the share price) of deals is only about 30 percent. The worst deals they found, and which we confirmed through additional analysis, are "big bang" transforming mergers (such as AOL-Time Warner, or Daimler-Chrysler) whose success rate we judge to be a paltry 5 to 10 percent.

Evidence from Shrinking Value Creators

Our final validation of the power of focusing on the profitable core comes from our analysis of the rare and transient group of shrinking value creators. These are the few companies (only 3 percent to 4 percent of our sustained value creators) whose real revenues shrank during the decade of our analysis but whose rates of value creation remained positive. Eighty-five percent of the shrinking value creators in our database followed the same formula: They shrank their company down to a subset of businesses clustered around an original core. One example is Sears, which decided to divest its financial services businesses as it was working to revive its core retail business. Another is General Dynamics, which undertook an extensive divestiture program. A third is Royal Vopak, a Dutch company in the marine oil and chemical storage business that shrunk its business in 2001 by more than 85 percent to its strongest core—and today is worth more than four times what it was when the company was about seven times larger!

What is especially striking about shrinking value creators is the extent to which the right answer for each involved shrinking in a way that restored the core business to its original status at the center. Consider Guinness, the Irish brewing business that stems back to 1759, when thirty-four-year-old Arthur Guinness leased a small disused brewery at St. James Gate on the outskirts of Dublin (at a rent of £45 per year for a nine-thousand-year term). In 1886, Guinness became the first brewery to be listed on the London Stock Exchange, and soon after, it became the largest brewer in the world.

After World War II, the Guinness family launched a major diversification program, entering no fewer than 250 other businesses. By the early 1980s, Guinness's growth had ground to a halt, and its equity in Stout, the smooth dark beer for which it is famous, was severely eroded. The company's only hope was to retrace its steps back to the core. So it embarked on an aggressive divestiture program and, during one eighteen-month period, sold more than 150 of its businesses. The liberated cash was reinvested in the beer business to automate systems, develop new products, rebuild the Guinness brand equity, and fuel international expansion. Over the next eight years, the company's stock price increased nearly ten thousand times (!), and in 1997 the company merged with Grand Metropolitan to become Diageo. Fortunately, Guinness returned to the profitable core before it was too late.

Exceptions to the Strong Core

This crystalline business form is a useful point of departure. Yet, while the data shows that market share dominance in a well-defined core business creates superior profitability, it does not address several more common situations.

First, it does not explain the historic success of many strong follower businesses such as American Express versus Visa in credit cards, Canon versus Xerox in copiers, Toyota versus GM in automotive, or Southwest versus United in airlines. Such an explanation requires a broader way of thinking about what types of market power and influence can achieve leadership economics without leading scale. Second, while the data emphasizes the importance of relative market share in well-defined businesses, it does not address the increasingly common situation of blurred and fuzzy business boundaries that make it extremely difficult to determine market share and relevant competitors. Just think of markets such as communication lines into the home, in which cable competes with phone lines competing with wireless competing with T1 lines, and so on. Or think of the newspaper industry whose competition was once no more complex than the other newspaper in town. Today, with information "unbundled" and on the Internet, there are new and separate competitors for virtually every category—stock quotations (Yahoo!), headlines (CNN.com), classifieds (Craigslist), weather (weather.com)—and the picture is further complicated by new delivery vehicles like Amazon's electronic book, the Kindle. What now is the right business definition and boundaries? No longer is it sufficient to keep track of only one set of similar competitors in a well-defined historical arena. No longer are you guaranteed a collegial industry association to collect and array market data, as was the case in industries such as steel and machine tools and typewriters. Today the equivalent industry association for each of these product groups would have ambiguous boundaries—if it existed.

The remainder of this chapter summarizes the key requirements for building a strong core as the foundation for growth strategy. For each, we provide some tools and suggest the most common sources of failure in the cases we studied.

Define the Business

Having a clear sense of business boundaries and of the definition of your core is a critical starting point for growth strategy. Are the boundaries stable or shifting? Which areas must be defended at all costs, and which are not strategic? From which areas will future profits likely spring, and from which will current profits likely diminish? What is the true source of differentiation and capability to win against competitors, and how might the shifting business boundaries demand changes in your core capabilities in order to compete in the future?

Perhaps the greatest danger in the companies we studied came from mistakes in defining the "core" correctly and determining the right definition of the appropriate boundaries in which it can reasonably compete. We have found that failing to do that correctly can lead to premature departures from the core and sometimes to disastrous misadventures in pursuit of businesses that should not have been pursued, and, in fact, whose pursuit even imperiled the original core itself.

Dell Computer, the top performer of the decade from 1990 through 1999 among large companies, departed from its core with a jolt and quickly returned. Dell grew rapidly from its initial public offering in 1988. In 1993 it decided to expand from its core of direct sales of computers by launching a sales program targeted at discount retailers and wholesale clubs. Shortly thereafter, the company began to lose money. It suffered a loss of $37 million on sales of $600 million in the third quarter of 1993. Michael Dell and his team quickly diagnosed the problem as the company's departure from its core strategy and "direct sales model" and its attempt to sell just like its competitors, through retailers. Although the retail program constituted only 10 percent of Dell's business at the time, it had a huge effect. The expansion eroded the core itself because of, as Michael Dell says today, "the confusion [it] injected into our strategy. Every major business decision in the core business was set against the question of what it would do to the unprofitable retail part of the business . . . When we realized this, we withdrew immediately. Even though it was painful and costly to do this, it was probably one of the defining moments for the company and saved us from disaster."[12]

The personal computer business in the early 1990s, the time of the Dell example, was growing at well over 20 percent each year and changing rapidly. It is no surprise that a small turn of the steering wheel could send the speeding vehicle of Dell briefly onto the shoulder of the road, shocking the driver into turning back onto the pavement. However, similar departures from the core can occur even in businesses that exist in much slower growth environments. No matter what your business or industry is, focusing on the core requires continual diligence.

The case of Hilti International provides a great example of the sustained, profitable growth that can emerge from refocusing on the core. Hilti was founded in 1941 by the brothers Martin and Eugen Hilti to commercialize their design of the DX nail gun for firing metal fasteners into concrete using a proprietary power-activated system. The company has since grown to nearly $1.8 billion as the leader in innovation in preformed drilling and fastening products.

During the early 1990s, Hilti found itself in an extended period of stagnant growth in an industry that has historically grown at less than 1 percent. The company responded by moving swiftly into a range of new products at the lower end of the market, including drill bits and fasteners, basic supplies, screws, and chemicals. This move brought an increase in revenue growth to 4 percent but also the unintended consequence of driving down profits and margins.

The Hilti family felt it was time for a more fundamental appraisal of its growth strategy. Examining every customer segment and product line in detail, management discovered that virtually all of the new lower-end products intended to increase sales per customer were unprofitable. It concluded that the company had moved prematurely away from its core competence of innovation in solving complex and specialized customer problems through new, highly engineered products and superior customer support. Indeed, a study at the University of Aachen during this time identified Hilti as being among the most innovative product companies in Southern Europe. For instance, Hilti developed the first drill with a vacuum surrounding its drill head to allow a mason to work without leaving a particle of dust on the floor.

Through initiatives of its CEO at the time, Dr. Pius Baschera, Hilti refocused on its core. Baschera called the company's new strategy Champion 3C (for customer, competency, and concentration). The result was investment in product innovation and even deeper specialized application of drilling and fastening, such as diamond coring mining (strenuous applications with high-risk and demanding technical specifications) as well as new ranges of premium products, such as for woodworking. At the same time, Hilti throttled back on the lower-end, marginal product lines. Its growth since the mid-1990s has been 9 percent in revenues and 14 percent in profits through increased geographic penetration and a burst of new technical products. Today the company is examining new growth initiatives once again for its core business in growing segments like the installation of solar panels. But this time, these extensions will cluster around the core of technical, highly engineered, premium products, leveraging the technical sales force and protecting the high-quality brand.

Setting the Right Boundaries

Without a clear point of view about business boundaries, it is difficult to determine competitive position, the relative importance of differently positioned competitors, or the relative strategic importance of different growth opportunities. To make the right decisions, it is critical to have a clear definition of your core business, the relevant business adjacencies that surround your core, and the competitive and economic landscape. The degree to which these adjacent areas are related to your own core is key to establishing your business offense and defense across the boundaries. Mapping out the territory should be the starting point of any growth strategy in business.

The profitable core is centered on your strongest position in terms of loyal customers, competitive advantage, unique skills, and the ability to earn profits. If you are not profitable in your core, except during the earliest phases of market development and start-up, something is probably wrong. Surrounding the core are the most promising adjacencies for expansion, where the skills of the core can be leveraged or where defensive moves are critical to protect core customers. But these moves require a strong core to build upon. The average "adjacency move" has a success rate, we find, of 20 to 25 percent. Adjacency moves off a strong core have nearly twice the success rate. And such moves, if "very close" to a well-defined core, can go even higher. Growth in many industries comes down to the ability to spot the right adjacency moves before your competitors, to execute them faster, and to achieve higher odds of success. In some competitive battles, such as the U.S. battle for athletic footwear between Nike and Reebok, a strong core with a repeatable formula to leverage into new adjacencies can be the defining reason why one company—Reebok—lapses into the background, while the other—Nike—emerges as the undisputed leader.

But, you might ask, aren't we supposed to remove boundaries, not add them, to come up with growth strategy? Aren't we supposed to think outside of the box, not in and around a definition? No. Misdefining the business (whether through poor judgment or plain sloppiness) commits you to invest in areas unlikely to lead to profitable growth or to ignore areas you should reinforce. Defining the business accurately is a way of creating a logical hierarchy of territories in and around your core business that help you target wise investments, stop investments that are out of bounds, and track market share, making profit comparisons with competitors.

Just think for a moment of playing tennis. If two competitors had different definitions of the court but only one was right, the one with the wrong definition would surely lose the game. He would either fire shots outside the true boundaries or hit to a narrow space that was too small, making it easier for his opponent to return the ball. If a pair of doubles players had different concepts of the court boundaries, chaos would ensue, and the team would quickly dissolve.

Consider the following actual growth strategy decisions that hinge on subtle and difficult issues of business definition:

• Is Coca-Cola in the cola business, the soft drink business, the beverage business, or some other business? Ample evidence suggests that Coke has defined its business success as share of liquid consumed, not share of cola, and that this definition has enlarged the company's sense of full potential and emboldened its investment strategy ("I'd like to buy the world a Coke") relative to competitors.

• Is the business definition of Google just the search engine and its logical adjacencies? Or does its strength and ability to compete extend into all searchlike arenas from maps to community networking? Will it one day extend its business to the distribution of information products (it is already digitally scanning all major books on the planet)? Or is it an advertising services provider, with a business that involves licensing its unique software to others (as it does with Yahoo! for searches)?

• Does a glass windshield manufacturer correctly define its business as supplying windshields? Or should it consider creeping into subsystem integration, adding to the tasks it performs on and around a windshield or glass side panel? Consolidation is rampant in the automobile parts industry, with more and more companies integrating and assembling systems of doors, seats, or electrical subsystems and expanding along their value chain. Here, business definition has a defensive application as well as offensive.

• Is Nokia in the business of providing ever more sophisticated handsets, or can its hardware business shift to software and services embedded in the phone as a distribution vehicle? For instance, in 2007 Nokia purchased NAVTEQ, one of the two leading geopositional map and data companies. This move brings it into direct competition with other types of devices such as TomTom's positioning product line. As Nokia's handset business starts to slow, and traffic on wireless phones shifts from voice to data, Nokia must redefine its business in a realistic and attainable way. How do moves like this redraw business boundaries and redefine the core?

- What must CBS do to strengthen its once nearly dominant core? Should it focus on content production; extend the core by creating and controlling the largest number of cable channels; reinvigorate CBS News to compete more vigorously with CNN, as NBC has tried to do through CNBC; or take some other tack? In the last five years, market share numbers for top networks have continued to slip to single-digit percentages of viewers who have a plethora of options. Which direction to choose? And how will the business definition, and the type of differentiation, shift in the future?

- On an even larger scale, how should AT&T define its business now that the methods by which voice messages are transmitted change and the transmission of data (a much bigger slice of the telecom infrastructure) escalates and moves from traditional phone lines to wireless, cable, private systems, and, most of all, the Internet? What, then, are the business definition and the core of AT&T as the promise of technology convergence continues to prove itself?

The need for a strong core business to support a growth strategy requires defining both what that business is and what it is not—and where it can compete versus where it cannot.

The Blurring of Business Boundaries

Without a clear and accurate point of view on the boundaries of your core business and how they might be changing over time, it is possible to make fatal growth-strategy mistakes. Throughout this book we caution that errors in defining a business are among the most frequent and most dangerous forms of strategic error. Yet today business boundaries are more difficult to determine and are changing more often than ever before.[13]

Our experience is that the size and scope of most core businesses that might establish significant competitive advantage are shrinking due to the use of outsourcing and customer segmentation specialists. At the same time, the area around any core business, the *adjacencies* of relevance for strategy, is growing substantially. Moreover, potential future competitors for your current core and future sources of control over the profitability (the *profit pool*) in your core business lie in these adjacencies.

Consider the following examples. For years, digital imagery was a document management technology at the boundary of Xerox's core copier business. But it took the advent of high-speed printers, combined with the power of new word processing software, for digital imagery to become both a threat to and a primary shaper of the future profit pool for Xerox. Or consider network TV news, long a tight oligopoly of three participants, with cable TV at the fringes. Today, the three networks have a minority share of news-related programming viewed on television and an even smaller share of the margin pool. Or think about the dynamics in the telephone business today. At what point will wireless cellular services become the same business as land lines? How will the continued evolution of Internet telephony affect the profit pools of both in a significant way? And what will this mean for the long-term definition of the telephone business and the sources of differentiation that will allow companies of the future to compete profitably?

These are three examples of large and increasingly important adjacencies around a once tightly defined core business. The blurring of boundaries and creation of larger arenas of relevance strategically around a core are being driven by a number of key trends that are likely to persist for the foreseeable future:

- Outsourcing and the disintegration of traditional value chains

- Increased customer microsegmentation and new, more narrowly focused competitors

- Increased competition among different business models rather than merely among versions of the same one

- Digital convergence blurring the boundaries between all information businesses

- Forces of globalization blurring regional geographic boundaries and increasing competitiveness

- Increasingly sophisticated supply chain strategies causing competition between supply chains as much as between companies

Defining the Core

Your own core business is defined by that set of products, customer segments, and technologies with which you can build the greatest competitive advantage. Defining the boundaries is as much a matter of making sound business judgments as of applying formulas or doing calculations.

A critical ingredient in formulating the right business definition is a clear understanding of your core customers and products that are expected to yield a majority of profit economics, or that have produced those economics historically. We are surprised at how often we find that members of management teams, when interviewed one on one, differ in their opinions of the core customer set and products. Your understanding of and consensus about the core can be sharpened by analyzing profit numbers and by mapping out the profit pool for this core business across direct competitors and customer segments.

Once you have an understanding of the right economics of the core customers and products that you are currently serving, you can then examine successive segments of the market radiating out from that core. In some complex markets, there may be as many as ten total segments. Each must be understood and prioritized for resources. In general, we find that the key strategic decisions are made in the inner core and in one or two other segments emanating from it.

Taking the personal computer business as an example, think of the following distinct areas of economic activity, all related to competition and growth in companies such as Dell, Lenovo, and Hewlett-Packard. These segments are listed from within the core PC business to the farthest out from the core, as best as that sort of ordering is possible:

1. Segments within the core (PCs sold to elementary school students in the United States)

2. The inner core itself (the global PC market)

3. Indirect competitors for computing (such as dumb terminals attached to a network)

4. Enhanced PC products (such as low-end servers and workstations)

5. Ancillary "computing" devices (appliances and handheld devices)

6. Complementary products but different businesses (software, software loading, Internet service providers, peripherals)

7. Product line extensions (storage devices, enhanced services)

8. Upstream supply chain activities (components, "cloud" computing, remote storage)

9. Downstream activities (retail, distribution)

10. Other businesses that could share costs with a PC business

Clearly, the majority of resources should be expended in defending and expanding the inner core of the PC business, in staving off new competitors at the boundaries, and in looking for complementary products and services to deepen customer relationships and increase spending per customer. However, it would be premature to define the business and develop strategy without considering the full profit pool of the PC industry, including supplier power, channel power, and the potential for new, disruptive technologies outside of traditional boundaries. Specific competitors might define their own inner core slightly differently, depending on their strengths. But the industry definition would be the same for all, emanating farther out into the previous list (items 4 through 9).

Defining an area as noncore, at least for a while, can be as valuable as defining an area as core. By taking a competitive arena off the agenda, you focus the organization and liberate attention and resources for the most important battles. Without such focus, organizations inherently tend to add segments and priorities. This is an especially costly tendency in successful businesses with a growing number of possible paths before them.

Defining the core obviously requires defining what is clearly irrelevant and what falls into the gray area that needs to be carefully monitored or anticipated. The key types of decisions that need to be anticipated in the gray areas, or so-called blurring boundaries, are these:

- Do I need to expand my definition to include a new segment or technology? If so, do I need to add it? If so, how?

- Are any of the competitive dynamics in the gray area likely to affect the profit pool in my core business? If so, how, and how should I react?

- Are any of the competitors that are not currently threatening likely to make incursions into my core customers? If so, what should I do?

- Are there capabilities or types of skills that I need to bring in-house now to be able to understand and, therefore, anticipate, some of the dynamics adjacent to my current core?

- Are there partnerships or alliances I could forge to insulate and stabilize my economic position surrounding my core?

Virtually every business has a core and an expanding and complex set of adjacencies. Defining the core is critical, but being extremely self-conscious and diligent about monitoring areas or competitors deemed temporarily to be noncore can be just as important to long-term, sustainable growth. As the examples and analyses in this book show, it is the balance between maintaining a strong core and adjusting to threats and opportunities in business adjacencies that is the central tension of growth strategy.

Differentiate for Unique Market Power and Influence

Successful differentiation creates lasting market power and influence over customers or competitors. This section discusses the traditional metric, relative market share, and then explores alternative sources of market power and influence, which sustained value creators are using to their benefit. The increasing potential for building substantial market power and influence in the absence of scale gives strong followers and new entrants a greater strategic edge than our data on stable industries might suggest, though they face a set of strict conditions for strong followership.

Traditional Measures and Sources of Market Power

Our analysis over the past two decades shows consistently that most of the sustained growth companies had achieved leadership in their core business, as measured by their market share relative to their next largest competitor. In spite of the recurrent talk about "new business models," and the many situations where market power can be protected in a niche, or is resident in new, small, and growing "challengers," relative share is still the predominant source of market power and the best single measure to start with. The original source of market power is not usually scale. Scale is a result of other forms of differentiation such as product development or channel control. In some sense, scale is an output of more fundamental competitive advantage in the core. Nonetheless, three-quarters of the most profitable companies in a competitive arena have superior relative market share. This differential drives, in most cases, superior cost and profits.

In an analysis of six hundred companies across more than eighty markets, we determined the average rate of profitability over the cost of capital as compared to relative market share. We found consistently that the average returns for companies with weak relative market share (less than 30 percent the size of the major competitor) was 16 points lower than for companies with relative market shares that were at least 2.5 times as big as their major competitors. Although relative market share has been criticized recently in business writings for being used as the sole measure of market power and influence, it nonetheless remains a significant measure in a large percentage of industries.

Relative market share clearly drives market influence, cost position, and resulting leadership economics in a wide range of businesses such as mass retail (Wal-Mart), package delivery (UPS), grocery (Tesco in the United Kingdom or Publix in the United States, for instance), and telecom (AT&T). We analyzed more systematically the core elements of the business models of leaders and found that in 60 percent of the cases, the most important source of market power was relative cost leadership, driving both pricing and reinvestment rate. In the other 40 percent, we also found that cost economics and relative scale were important in half of those cases. However, there are clearly many businesses in which market power and relative competitive performance is driven heavily by the ability to create differentiated products with consumer appeal at a superior rate (P&G, Apple, and BMW would be examples here), and a few cases in which the key was to establish a commanding position as a physical "control point" in a market (the classic example would be the Microsoft operating system for PCs). And, of course, sometimes a business begins and grows with a highly differentiated business model that, with growth and development, begins to achieve economies of scale and capture more traditional sources of leadership economics and cost position

(Amazon.com and Nike might be examples of such an evolution in the source of leadership economics).

Developing Market Power and Influence

In examining the source of market power for the top one hundred small companies as well as for a sample of our sustained value creators, we found four basic ways that companies acquire market power and influence in a competitive arena in a core business and thereby drive scale. These are arrayed in figure 2-2. All of these methods are available to all businesses—those that are followers and those that are leaders. A company considering its growth strategy should ask itself which of these is the true underlying source of power and influence.

Customer Loyalty. The most robust form of market power derives from building a uniquely high and structurally stable level of loyalty in a well-defined customer segment. A mere 5 percent increase in the retention of a credit card company's best customers could lead to a value creation increase of 75 percent. This increase comes from

Customer-Based	Channel-Based	Product- or Capability-Based	Capital-Based
• Superior service and relationship (loyalty) • High switching costs • Superior information on behavior/ needs • Business model built around new segment	• Channel dominance • Partnership with leading channel participants • Control point in a network	• Low-cost production • Superior/unique features • New-to-world products • Patents • Deep share of wallet	• High valuation, creating acquisition currency • Capital availability, allowing companies to outinvest competitors

2-2 Companies Acquire Market Power and Influence in Many Ways

extending the lifetime value from capturing a new customer and from realizing the permanent increase in growth rate from a change in retention and loyalty. Because increases in retention stop growth from "running out the bottom of the bucket," a growing company can magnify its rate of growth by 5 to 10 percentage points by effecting a permanent, one-time increase in retention. Few improvements in a business can have this impressive impact on sustained profitable growth.

Customer loyalty can be built as a competitive advantage in an existing customer segment, as USAA has done in the case of insuring the needs of current and former members of the military services. Today, USAA has more than a 96 percent retention rate of this population, a 94 percent satisfaction rating, and it sells an average of more than four separate products to each of its customers, an almost unheard of share-of-wallet performance. USAA systematically tracks each customer through twenty-three life stages, carefully choreographing its marketing and sales programs around these events of greatest propensity to purchase.[14] The achievement of market power and influence through customer loyalty in these instances comes from switching cost to the customer in tandem with offering superb customer service and depth of knowledge.

The other way to build market power and influence through customer segment focus and loyalty is by identifying or even creating a totally new customer segment and dominating its experience of a product or service. Starbucks coffee grew during the 1990s at a 55 percent annual rate as compared with a mere 1.3 percent growth in coffee consumption. Starbucks serves eight million customers per week, who average an amazing eighteen visits per month to its stores. Customers commonly drive five miles to buy their cup of Starbucks coffee. On the surface, the pharmaceutical effect of the strong, rich brew seems an easy explanation for this loyalty. However, other companies' coffee is strong too. The lure comes from a carefully orchestrated combination of product, ambience, and ubiquity. Certainly, many other companies, such as Nestlé, had the idea and the ability to develop a chain of coffeehouses, but none used their leadership to do so. Starbucks' market power and influence is made potent by scale but did not begin with scale. It is interesting to see recent difficulties at Starbucks resulting in the return of the founder to the helm of the company, commenting that he believed that the essence of the company's core had been diluted and compromised over time—and vowing a return to the original core values and customer practices that drove its original success.

For instance, Fred Reichheld has, in a series of books over the past decade, documented the many ways that the economics of customer loyalty work. Central to a strong core are almost always a cadre of loyal core customers. For instance, we have found strong supporting evidence in the fact that the one-in-ten businesses that we defined as sustained value creators (SVCs) earlier in chapter 1 not only tended to exploit leadership economics in their core business, but also had customer advocacy scores that were, on average, 15 to 20 percentage points higher than the scores of non-SVC companies. Reichheld, in his most recent book *The Ultimate Question*, provides compelling data on the economic value of these strong core customers—he refers to them as advocates. In industry after industry, the driving force behind a strong core business is a far-above average percentage of these customer advocates.[15] Examples of companies with exceptionally high percentages of "promoters" in their customer base would include Walgreens (55 percent), USAA (94 percent), Costco (81 percent), and AFLAC in health insurance (47 percent).

Channel Dominance. Establishing leadership in a new or existing channel of product or service distribution is the second most common model of building market power and influence, sometimes from a position of followership. This is not a new discovery. It is how Venice transformed from a fishing village to the wealthiest city in Europe in the 1400s through its control of the channel by which spices and tea were then reaching the West.

Channel leadership is also how Dell Computer Company established its market power in the 1990s (the "growth stock of the decade" according to the *Wall Street Journal*) and went from start-up to global leader in PCs and workstations. Computer components, and even assembled computers, were available by mail order well before Dell was formed. However, no one saw the potential for the direct channel to gain share as clearly as Michael Dell did. Selling direct, rather than through layers of distributors, value-added resellers, and retail intermediaries (the way Compaq and IBM were selling their computers at the time), had powerful economic advantages: lower cost due to fewer layers and middleman markups, lower pipeline inventory and fresher (higher-margin) components on average because of a six- versus seventy-day inventory pipeline, and a distribution channel tailored in cost and service to each customer segment. The brilliance of developing this channel was not only its lower cost but also its potential for higher customer service and, as luck would later have it, its ability to be turbocharged by the Internet. The natural structural advantage that this direct channel conferred during this growth phase of the PC industry was 10 percent to 15 percent over most competitors at one-tenth the inventory and capital levels.

The Internet provided many companies with the potential in their industry to enter and gain market power and influence in the new channel of online sales. Charles Schwab has used the Web brilliantly to bootstrap itself from a follower in the securities and financial management market to consumers to the clear leader. We estimate that Schwab has three times relative market share of online trading volume and captures a hefty 70 percent of the online profit pool. Compare that with its share of profit in traditional channels, which we estimate to be about 12 percent.

Product Development Differentiation. The power of differentiation through superior product development is the rarest form of market power and influence in our sample of sustained value creators. Our analysis of the sustained value creators indicates that fewer than 5 percent rely primarily on this method. However, those companies that do build superior product development engines often are able to enter new markets, dominated by incumbents, and to gain market share profitably.

The entertainment industry—both recording artists and devices—has long been one where such differentiation is paramount. For instance, ten years ago, in 1999, Sony was a $63 billion company with revenues growing at a rate of 13.9 percent in 1996 through 1999 and profits at an astounding rate of 48.9 percent. It had a long history, since its founding in 1946 as a consumer electronics company, of growing by leveraging a stream of innovative products. Its first challenge, from cofounder Masaru Ibuka, was to create Japan's first pocket-sized radio. This deep and strong business core has adapted throughout the ensuing half century. For example, Sony entered the television business in 1968 and rapidly outgrew much larger competitors with its Trinitron televisions, due to their superior clarity and color quality. Today, the Sony TV is the standard of the industry. Another example: In 1995, Sony took on Sega and Nintendo in the home video game station market and emerged with leading market share—for a while. Ultimately, it lost position to Nintendo when the latter came out with the Wii, offering a remarkable advance in interactivity due to its unique user interface, a product feature unrelated to historic scale, and one that swept leadership away in less than a year from its launch. In a similar dramatic fashion, Sony lost its position to Apple in small music players (where the Walkman was the early pioneer). By early 2008, Apple had taken more than 71 percent of the market for portable music players with its iPod; products from Sony no longer even made it onto most market-share charts—great testimony to the power of product features and user interfaces in a global manufacturing business.

Access to Capital. Though it does not focus on the topic, this book would be incomplete if it did not at least mention the market power that occurs when one competitor has access to capital (or very low cost capital) and others do not. Over the past decade we have seen this play out in several distinct ways for businesses whose "core" included a privileged access to capital. One way that access to capital has been core to competitive advantage has been in developing economies. Often, developing economies have higher risk premiums and more challenging access to capital for large projects or acquisitions. Those circumstances, over the years, have given rise to a wide range of conglomerate forms such as the *chaebol* of Korea, where access to capital was a key core advantage. The second way that access to capital has conferred competitive advantage is in situations such as the global financial crisis of 2008–2009 where liquidity dried up. Businesses in these situations such as the large private equity firms, sovereign wealth funds, and companies with strong leadership positions and cash flows will find that privileged capital access is a core competitive advantage compared to rivals, permitting moves that have enormous competitive implications in the longer term.

Seek the Full Potential Value of a Strong Core

Our argument so far can be summarized as follows: Few companies grow and create value sustainably over periods even as short as ten years. Those that do so tend to focus on one, or at most two, core businesses in which they are clearly the leader or, in the rare cases of the strong followers, in which they manage to simulate the economic conditions that accrue to market leadership. These economic conditions and market power give companies higher profitability, greater control over the extended industry profit pool, and tighter control over investable capital in their competitive arenas. Typically, as in the obvious cases of Coca-Cola, Intel, Cisco, Wal-Mart, UPS, Toyota, Tesco, SAP, or Microsoft, the continued application of economic leadership leads first to growth that outstrips that of others in the industry and then to "traditional" scale leadership. For instance, two-thirds of our sustained value creators grew more rapidly than their industry averages and were thereby gaining share in their marketplaces. In fact, the average sustained value creator in our database grew twice as rapidly as its industry in revenues and more than three times as rapidly in total profits. The question naturally arises, then, since most companies are followers, how can they gain market power and simulate leadership economics?

Throughout the discussions of sustained value creation, we have indicated our strong belief that many companies have, or once had, the right ingredients but somehow failed to recognize the potential of their profitable core. This failure has led companies to underinvest in the core, to set performance targets that are too low (leading to undermanagement), or to abandon the core prematurely for seemingly greener pastures in new or hotter industries. Companies consistently have a built-in bias, it seems, toward underestimating three dimensions of the core:

1. Increasing returns to leadership, leading to higher profits

2. Influence over investable funds, leading to competitive advantage

3. Influence over the extended industry profit pool, leading to access to superior profit growth opportunities in adjacent businesses

Increasing Returns to Market Leadership

How much should my business be earning? Where should I set profit and return on investment targets and expectations for management? These are critical questions that every CEO must answer every year. And many get the answers wrong by failing to recognize both the full potential of their core business and the potential for increasing returns on their investment in their core business's market position. In doing so, managers set targets that are too low, develop investment plans that are too modest, achieve growth that is too low, watch market share trajectories flatten, and give competitors incentive to invest more.

Just how strong are increasing returns in the core? The answer varies by industry and competitive situation. However, the general pattern can be seen by returning to our cross-sectional database. Our findings, plotted in figure 2-3, indicate that companies near parity

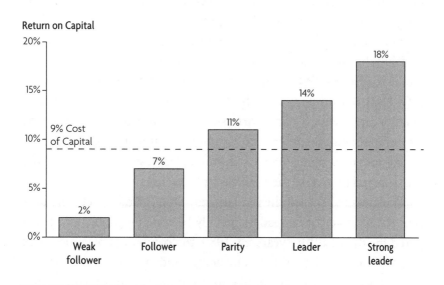

2-3 Market Leadership Drives Increasing Returns

Source: CapitalIQ database; Bain case experience; Bain analysis.

Note: Return on Capital defined as EBIT*(1-tax rate)/(net working capital + net property, plant and equipment + goodwill). Average of 600+ companies in 80+ different markets. Leader/follower position determined based on size relative to largest competitor.

with their competitors earned an 11 percent return on capital. Market leaders, however, achieved a 14 percent return on capital, and strong market leaders saw that percentage rise to an impressive 18.

Clearly, a leader can earn ten to fifteen points or more above its industry average and gain market share at the same time. Dell Computer has earned a 200 percent return on capital while growing at a rate three to four times the industry average.

An example of a company that built an exceptionally strong leadership position and failed, for a time, to recognize its full profit potential is the Dun & Bradstreet Credit Services business. This business has roots in the early 1800s, when letters of reference from local bankers and prominent citizens such as clergymen were used to encourage businesspeople to extend credit to traders. The system worked well in small, local markets where community members knew one another, but as the U.S. economy grew, the method no longer sufficed. Moreover, the depression of 1837 saw more than six hundred banks fail, further heightening the anxiety of lenders and highlighting the need for a reliable method of establishing creditworthiness. Shortly thereafter, two companies were founded, R.G. Dun & Company and the John M. Bradstreet Company. For nearly a century these rivals skirmished, with both growing in tandem and suppressing the other's profitability so that neither gained a lasting competitive edge. In 1933, as the Great Depression came to a close, they merged to reverse their increasingly tenuous profit outlook.

Such was the core of the modern-day Dun & Bradstreet Corporation. The merger of co-leaders quickly became profitable and prospered for the next fifty years. By 1980, the company's revenues were $1.2 billion, of which the credit business contributed about $500 million. This credit business, unlike its component parts of the earlier century, had a relative market share of more than six times that of its nearest commercial credit rival, had an 11.2 percent operating margin, and generated $56 million in profits, placing it well within the upper echelon of U.S. business performance. Yet, the following decade would prove that the business was still underperforming.

Under a new CEO and COO, the company reevaluated its credit business and concluded that this profitable core was operating below its full profit and growth potential. Over the next few years, the business increased its reinvestment rate, computerized its database, introduced new marketing concepts into its data packaging, increased its data quality and pricing, and added voice and online distribution services. By 1990, sales in the credit business had doubled to nearly $1 billion, the operating margin had expanded by nearly threefold to 28.2 percent, and profits had grown to $269 million. Even in 2008, after waves of new information technologies affecting the business, D&B's credit business remains the market leader with high margins, leadership economics, and an ability and incentive to continually outinvest its competitors.

What is important here is not the company's exact strategy but the amount of gold available to be mined in its core business with origins predating the Civil War. The Dun & Bradstreet case illustrates the hidden value of a strong core business and our strong but counterintuitive finding that the better performing your business, the more likely it is performing below its full potential.

Influencing Industry Reinvestment

Drilling down into twenty competitive pairings, we analyzed the extent to which our sustained value creators outinvest their competitors in their core business. We estimated reinvestment rate as the sum of capital expenditures, research and development, and advertising relative to sales. The sustained value creators invested at a rate of 15.3 percent, nearly twice that of their rivals, at 8.7 percent. Relative reinvestment is one reason that two-thirds of our sustained value creators grew at a significantly higher rate than their industry averages over the ten years we tracked. We find in our consulting work for large corporations that relative reinvestment rate is poorly tracked and analyzed, yet it embodies a great deal of information about an industry's future and competitive dynamics. Planning a strategy without collecting and interpreting competitor reinvestment rates is like forecasting the weather without looking at wind speed or temperature.

Consider the well-known case of Intel from the perspective of its historic focus on the core and relative reinvestment levels and rate. In 1980, Intel was smaller in total market value than either Advanced Micro Devices or National Semiconductor. Today, Intel's market value is more than twenty times that of the combined total of AMD and National Semiconductor. Since 1984, AMD and National Semiconductor have seen their stock prices rise and fall precipitously.

Part of the story is that in the 80s and 90s Intel narrowed its strategic focus and simultaneously adopted a preemptive reinvestment strategy. Intel, investing at the same rate as its rivals in 1984, narrowed its investment focus (from memory, chip sets, and integrated logic circuits down to just logic chips). It also turbocharged its rate of spending on new, low-cost manufacturing capacity and new products (such as the 486 family of chips). Its spending over that period ramped up from an average of $300 million per year to $2 billion per year by 1992 to more than $7 billion in 2000. By contrast, AMD and National Semiconductor's spending, as they fell farther behind, hovered at $500 million to $1 billion per year.

Looking back, a former director of the Intel microprocessor business whom we interviewed, reflected:

> During the early 1980s, most semiconductor companies were trying to be all things to all people. We decided to take a different course, exiting the memory business and focusing all of our efforts on the development of digital logic chips for the PC. Our core investment principle became "It had to serve the mother ship," which was the microprocessor business, or it would not get funded. For the next fifteen years, we steadily ramped up our level of investment relative to competition while at the same time narrowing down, avoiding all diversification except that which clearly reinforced the core.[16]

About this strategic reversal the online investment adviser Motley Fool commented:

> Watching Intel and AMD [Advanced Micro Devices] battle is almost like watching the Harlem Globetrotters play the old Washington Generals. The Globetrotters (Intel) needed the Generals (AMD) in order to play the game . . . but . . . there was never much doubt who would end up winning the game.[17]

Influencing the Extended Industry Profit Pool

Every profitable core business can be thought of as situated at the center of a complex network connecting direct suppliers, suppliers' suppliers, direct customers, customers' customers, complementary products, substitute products, competitors, and so on. Michael Porter has elegantly depicted these interconnections in many of his writings on strategy and positioning.[18] At the end of each of these economic connections is, usually, a pool of economic surplus and profit. The extent to which a company possesses the power of leadership in its core business influences the degree to which it can shape or even share in these profit pools adjacent to its own core business.

This concept may sound abstract, yet it is anything but. The ripple effects that Wal-Mart can project throughout its extended network of suppliers, and their suppliers, and their suppliers, are of primary strategic concern to those suppliers whose profits rise and fall with the moves and favor of a single customer. The ability of Coca-Cola to enter and influence, with ease, other soft drink categories—and even the bottled water business—shows how leadership provides adjacent growth opportunities not as readily available to followers. Thus, the third hidden value of market leadership is the ability to shape the profit pool and to project its power and influence into attractive adjacent businesses.

Take the case of W. W. Grainger, a company founded in 1927 that has become the nation's leading business-to-business distributor of small parts and industrial supplies for maintenance and repair. Grainger offers more than two hundred thousand products, from air circulators, engines, fans, and generators to hand tools and test instruments, to serve the needs of diverse markets, including commercial, industrial, contractor, and institutional customers. All products are available through online ordering or local branches. Grainger has 350 branches throughout the United States and Puerto Rico. In fact, 70 percent of all U.S. businesses are within twenty minutes of a Grainger branch.

Throughout the 1970s, Grainger grew profitably at 11 percent per year. Suddenly, in 1980, the business slowed to a 2 percent growth rate, which persisted to 1985. The attractive stock price growth of the company slumped, and profits per product in stock began to decline. At issue was whether Grainger—three to four times larger and more profitable than its nearest competitors—had hit the expansion limits of its industry. In its traditional markets, products, and geographies, its market share could be calculated to be as high as 40 percent. Moreover, industrial distribution busi-nesses are notorious for being populated by mom-and-pop com-petitors that can operate on thin margins for a long time. Was Grainger's core business expansion over?

The company embarked on a major project to determine its full growth potential and barriers to achieving it. What it discovered was that it had underassessed the full potential of its core business by a factor of ten! What it had believed to be a $3 billion market for its core business was actually a $30 billion potential market. Grainger found that density of stores drove relative market share and profitability and that it could add many more stores in its tradi-tional geographies. Adding stores lowered customers' travel time to the branches and dramatically increased sales. Moreover, Grainger had traditionally focused on specialized industrial buyers and spe-cialized products—particularly electronics and electrical parts. Yet, the Grainger branch structure and customer name recognition of 85 percent could be parlayed into sales of a wider range of products to a wider range of customers, at a low incremental cost. The com-pany could now sell a complete product line to its traditional core of customers. Together, the greater geographic density of stores and higher share of wallet lowered costs, increased the ability to invest in core customers, and improved service levels.

Grainger quickly identified and attacked its full-potential gaps with dramatic results. The company's revenues grew consistently and with growing profitability from $1.1 billion in 1985 to $4.8 bil-lion in 1999 to $6.9 billion by the end of 2008—a rate of 8 percent, nearly twice the underlying industrial rate of growth for the basic supply products that Grainger sells. During this period, Grainger doubled its reinvestment rate, increased its profit margin, and increased by a factor of ten the potential market its strong core busi-ness was going after. Grainger's example is yet another testament to the power of a focused core with leadership economics in a market with a range of possible adjacencies for growth.

Define the Profitable Core

In our experience, business definition is one of the most frustrating activities for senior executives. Although business leaders know that they should have a clear answer to the question, "What is our core business?" it is difficult to arrive at a fully satisfying statement. Part of the problem arises from blurring several distinct but related topics that need to be considered one at a time and then integrated in a consistent manner or within a single framework. In working toward a useful business definition, executives need to ask themselves the following questions:

1. What are the boundaries of the business in which I participate, and are those boundaries "natural" economic boundaries defined by customer needs and basic economics? What products, customers, channels, and competitors do these boundaries encompass?

2. What are the core skills and assets needed to compete effectively within that competitive arena?

3. What is my own core business as defined by those customers, products, technologies, and channels through which I can earn a return today and can compete effectively with my current resources?

4. What is the key differentiating factor that makes me unique to my core customers?

5. What are the adjacent areas around my core, and are the definitions of my business and my industry likely to shift, changing the competitive and customer landscape?

To illustrate the distinctness of these questions, consider a well-known business and product like Enterprise Rent-A-Car. The business in which Enterprise participates is the car rental market, including business, leisure, small-fleet leasing, and auto replacement in the event of an accident. Over the years, Avis and Hertz have also built up skills and assets in fleet management, reservations, pricing yield management, branch networking, and cost management that allow them to compete effectively in the rental car business. The core business of Enterprise, however, is probably the insurance replacement segment of the market, where it has more than 70 percent market share and where its original business began and from which it is now branching out. The differentiators for Enterprise are its low-cost business system, its ability to work with insurance companies and body shops, and its ability to move cars and customers to one another. The adjacent areas around the core once included airport and leisure rentals and even leasing, but for a variety of structural reasons in the industry, these boundaries now seem to be blurring.

A similar logic can be followed in any business. Just think of some companies that you commonly encounter, such as McDonald's in fast foods or Google in online search, and play out the questions for yourself. None of them is easy to answer. All must be informed by answering the umbrella question, "What is my core business?"

Companies whose cores map perfectly to the "natural boundaries" of the business, that possess competitive advantage, and that are in an industry where the boundaries are not poised to change discontinuously are in great shape. Many of the companies in our list of sustained value creators fit this pattern across several decades during which we have been performing this analysis on our global database of more than eight thousand companies. A more complex situation arises when the natural industry boundaries are quite different from a company's core business, creating either an unstable positioning or the need to develop a protected niche within a larger arena where larger companies prowl around the periphery of your core. One example is USAA in insurance, where the core is financial products for former military personnel and where the business thrives between behemoths such as Fidelity for investment and Allstate for insurance. Another is FootJoy in golf shoes, with Nike on one side and shoe companies on the other.

Conclusion

Achieving sustained and profitable growth is extremely difficult without having at least one strong and differentiated core business on which to build. The most enduring growth pattern is that of the strong, or dominant, core business that benefits from continual reinvestment, constant adaptation to circumstances or business environment, and persistent leveraging into new markets or geographies, applications, or channels.

The three crucial first steps for a management team developing, refining, or reexamining its company's growth strategy are outlined in this chapter: (1) Define the business boundaries and your own core business; (2) identify and verify the sources of differentiation that will continue to create market power and influence over your customers, competitors, and industry profit pool; and (3) comb through the core and assess whether it is operating at or near its full economic potential. Recall that the first paradox of growth is that the strongest core businesses are typically underperforming the most relative to their full potential.

3

The Alexander Problem

The tension between focusing on the core and setting out for new territory is universal and transcends business phenomena, spanning the affairs of nations to how to live one's life. The resolution of this tension is also the trigger point for many of the greatest blunders and most brilliant choices leaders have made in the history of business—or for that matter, all history.

Alexander the Great ruled the largest area of the earth ever conquered by a single individual, stretching from Mount Olympus to Mount Everest. Although not everyone's idea of the model CEO, he amassed his kingdom in less than four years, covering more than four thousand miles by foot, and winning 100 percent of his battles—a remarkable record in such a short time. But did he create *lasting* value? Just a few years after his death, his empire had dissolved and the captured territory slipped away. Alexander's problem was not inadequate initial resources or poor execution. It was the lack of a long-term strategy and the inability to exploit and consolidate his extraordinary short-term gains throughout the Near East to Nepal, which stretched resources to govern too far beyond the Macedonian core.

His sticking point—the failure to anchor in the core business (in his case, governance) and consolidate a rapid expansion—exemplifies the most common problem across all growth strategy. Our analysis of the growth paths of sustained value creators compared with those of their competitors indicates that the selection of new business adjacencies around the core business is the decision that most often triggers either a new burst of profitable growth or distraction and stagnation.

Embodied in this decision is a fundamental tension between protecting and investing in the core business, on the one hand, and expanding into adjacencies, on the other. The way companies resolve the tension often determines the sustainability of their growth.

This chapter focuses on the second element of our growth strategy, adjacency expansion from the core. We examine three topics critical to improving the odds of profitable, sustainable growth:

1. Identifying adjacent business opportunities and recognizing the most common patterns

2. Assessing and choosing the right adjacencies

3. Avoiding some common pitfalls of adjacency expansion

We also indicate how some typical views of adjacency expansion need to be adapted to today's turbulent business environment, with its increasingly blurred business boundaries.

Adjacency Expansion

Adjacency expansion is a company's continual moves into related segments or businesses that utilize and, usually, reinforce the strength of the profitable core. Over time, these sequenced moves can fundamentally redefine the core business (by adding new capabilities) as well as provide growth in themselves. Indeed, it is through adjacency expansion that a company in a stable industry repositions itself to go after the most attractive new profit pools or to respond to new environmental conditions.

Business adjacencies are growth opportunities that allow a company to extend the boundaries of its core business. What distinguishes an adjacency from another growth opportunity is the extent to which it draws on the customer relationships, technologies, or skills in the core business to build competitive advantage in a new, adjacent competitive arena. Examples of companies seizing adjacency opportunities range from UPS's move from package delivery into logistics, to Google's leap from the search engine business into Google Maps, to InBev's aggressive expansion into the United States by acquiring Anheuser-Busch.

Many of the most successful companies that we describe throughout this book are in industries within which lie extremely rich adjacencies. Diagrams of the step-by-step growth patterns of these companies often look like the concentric rings on the cross section of a decades-old tree. Adjacency-driven growth patterns are at the heart of the sustained, profitable growth of companies such as Tesco, Tetra Pak, Grainger, Microsoft, Intel, Dell, and Disney. Consider the following examples from American Express, Nike, and Dell.

American Express has grown by expanding its core business for more than 150 years. At the core of the original American Express company was a money order that could compete with the government's postal money order. The difficulty of extending this service into Europe spawned American Express's marquee product, the Travelers Cheque, in 1891. Travel-related payment systems have been at the heart of the company's adjacency expansion path through its launches of the American Express charge card in 1958 and the Optima revolving charge card in 1987 to the acquisition of more than 4,500 automated teller machines from Electronic Data Systems in 2000.

As with any 150-year growth record around a core business, not all has gone smoothly. American Express moved beyond its range of natural business adjacencies when it purchased Shearson Loeb Rhodes in 1981 and when it added Lehman Brothers investment banking house to the mix in 1984. One reporter said of this initiative, "After endless name changes and suffering the financial agonies of the damned, American Express decided to cut its losses and slink away . . . American Express will have blown more than $1 billion, not to mention endless hours of management time and years of lost investment opportunities."[1]

Investors have supported the company's return to its core. Today, American Express has applied a powerful, repeatable formula for adjacency expansion in many areas, such as online with its Blue Card, where it is the leading payment source online, or with small business owners with its new Plum card, where it offers special terms to that customer segment. Under the direction of CEO Ken Chenault, the company posted revenues of $22.4 billion, continued to grow earnings profitably and sustainably at a 16 percent rate, and attained a 37 percent return on equity around its original core just before the onset of the global financial crisis late in 2007.

Now consider the strategy that Nike has used to achieve an average 40 percent compound rate of growth since its founding as Blue Ribbon Sports in 1964. Nike has not relied solely on the core for growth but rather has developed a strong core and then repeatedly reignited slowing growth by finding the next logical, large-scale adjacency in which to leverage its strengths.

Nike's growth pattern reflects successive and distinct waves of adjacency expansion. From 1976 to 1983, Nike focused on its running shoe core to grow sales at an annual rate of 80 percent. But the running shoe business slowed to zero growth, on average, from 1983 to 1987. In the next era, 1987 to 1991, Nike surged powerfully by extending its running franchise into new product segments, including clothing, and rekindled growth to 36 percent per year, only to slow to 8 percent in 1991 to 1994. From 1994 to 1997, the company refocused on its athletic shoe business with emphasis on celebrity endorsements, especially the Air Jordan line, which exceeded $1 billion in sales in June 2009. Its growth has been fueled again by Nike's expansion into adjacencies such as golf and soccer. Nike's entrance into golf is epitomized by Tiger Woods's switch to the Nike golf ball for the 2000 U.S. Open at Pebble Beach, California, which he won by a record fifteen strokes.

Nike's up-and-down pattern is more extreme than the norm among our sustained value creators. Take soccer. When the United States hosted the World Cup in 1994, Nike's soccer revenues were only $45 million. Today, using its strong core and powerful repeatable formula, it has passed rival Adidas in some key product categories in the latter's home turf, Europe; grown to more than $5.6 billion in revenues; and acquired Umbro, an iconic U.K. company with a deep soccer heritage and relationships. Nike offers a striking example of how growth from the core can flag, creating the need to reignite new growth by shifting resources into nearby adjacencies. These adjacencies in turn build off a strong core—and the repeatable formula defines the way that the company takes its core strengths and applies them to new adjacent market opportunities.

Dell Computer's detailed growth path illustrates simultaneous expansion along multiple vectors: geography, products, customer segments, and ancillary services. The company began with direct phone sales of personal computers to medium-sized businesses in the United States. Since the early 1990s, it has expanded geographically to its present position as a fully global company with standard global products. It has expanded its products to increasingly highly engineered offerings, from PCs to laptops to workstations to servers to storage. It has also expanded into adjacent customer segments, from business to education to local government to multinationals, each segment served by a tailored and distinct selling protocol, cost structure, profit-and-loss profile, management team, and business model. It has expanded its ancillary services that ride along with the basic "boxes," from software loading to asset tagging to Internet services to consulting. Not all industries allow this logical, crystalline structure of adjacency expansion; the world is usually not so linear and geometric. However, in the case of Dell it was, propelling Dell to one of the best performance records of the 1990s.

Expansion into logical adjacencies around a core business is an offensive strategy, but it also has defensive implications. Building a profitable cushion around your core business can help to keep new invaders away or to block a sequence of a competitor's moves that lead into your core. Microsoft's entry into the game console business against Sony and Sega was heralded by the popular press at the time as "a radical departure from its core business."[2] If the consoles were perceived as hardware products with game cartridges, this observation would certainly have been true. However, the Sony strategy in home networking included positioning its PlayStation product as a potential computing hub for the home. *Wired* called PlayStation 2 "a platform so robust it may be all the computer some gamers and their families will ever need," describing it as a potential part of an array of home devices that "all talk to one another in a no-PC-required home network."[3] The challenges to realizing this potential primarily involve software, not hardware. And for that reason, not entering the home game console business would potentially have left one of Microsoft's software flanks exposed to a new competitor.

Alexander Revisited

The tension between expanding the boundaries of a business, in the presence of success and seeming invincibility, and maintaining the original core is at the center of our earlier-described "Alexander problem." Alexander's string of victories, won by thinly stretched and tired troops traveling from Athens to India, is extraordinary. At each stage, his forces faced the choice to stop and consolidate or to press on into more and more distant and unfamiliar territory. They consistently chose the latter and appeared to have won. Yet did they really win?

Consider these examples of companies that pursued unfamiliar adjacencies and failed to turn back to their core business in time to avoid serious damage:

- In 1994, Quaker Oats attempted to build on its Gatorade drinks business by purchasing the sparkling fruit juice company Snapple for $1.7 billion. The result was major internal disruption for several years and the eventual resale of Snapple at a $1 billion loss. In reality, there was less synergy between Gatorade and Snapple than management had believed. The sparkling juice company constituted not an adjacency but a diversification.

- For a decade, the United Kingdom's National Westminster Bank expanded aggressively into the United States. But the bank encountered tougher U.S. competition than its executives had forecast. In the end, NatWest decided to sell its U.S. business to Fleet at a loss, not only having lost money in the United States but also having slowed progress in its core British market.

- In the 1980s, Saatchi & Saatchi embarked on a major program of buying professional service firms, consultancies, a public relations firm, and other supporting businesses in an attempt to create a "one-stop shopping" experience for its customers. But customers did not value Saatchi's bundling, and the company incurred seven years of losses. The expansion strategy constituted diversification, which destroyed value by causing a loss of focus on the core.

- Under new management and with a new growth strategy, Gucci drove aggressively into apparent product adjacencies in lower-priced canvas goods sold through mass channels such as department stores and duty-free shops. The company also licensed its name for products ranging from watches to perfumes. Sales grew, but profits collapsed. The Gucci brand eroded. The company had expanded into shallow profit pools and diluted its core franchise. Gucci finally returned to its core and pruned the new, unprofitable growth.

- In the 1980s, Anheuser-Busch bought Eagle Snacks in an apparently logical adjacency expansion. People eat snacks with beer. Some snacks are sold where beer is sold, and the same trucks could sometimes carry both. Yet these potential synergies never materialized. Frito-Lay controlled the profit pool in the salty-snacks business and, implicitly, in Eagle's profits. In 1997, having seen $120 million in cash flow out during a time that its core beer business was slowing too, Anheuser-Busch ended its adjacency misadventure by divesting Eagle to Frito-Lay. Of course, in 2008 Anheuser-Busch was acquired by InBev, now the largest beer company in the world.

Even the best companies continue to expand into unknown territory, despite mounting evidence of strategic and execution risks in so doing. And even great companies can lose their way in the midst of a hailstorm of possible adjacencies that pummel them with greater speed and power as the firms grow larger and more successful.

Mattel, for instance, decided to enter the software business in 1999, buying The Learning Company for $3.8 billion. At the time, The Learning Company was a strong, growing business that was the clear leader in educational software. Yet the investment community was skeptical. The Learning Company exhibited slowing growth, and its cash flow from operations had declined to negative $43 million. Mattel pressed ahead, saying, "We are truly excited about the benefits to be realized through the combination of our two great companies."[4] But software is in many ways a difficult business, and a true departure from the toy business. After the acquisition, The Learning Company's performance eroded to a quarterly after-tax loss of $100 million. Reporting on the aftermath, the *New York Times* said:

> Mattel's woes illustrate the obvious but often overlooked fact that not all corporate marriages are created equal. Some are wise; others are breathtakingly foolish. . . . With more mergers taking place—the dollar amount of combinations worldwide is up 24 percent from last year, according to Thomas Financial Securities Data—investors need to be on the lookout for disasters.[5]

Mattel announced its exit from the software business one year after entering it, selling it for a price of zero.

Another company with a mixed adjacency-expansion record is Gillette. Gillette is one of the great global brand names, having built a 70 percent market share and brand dominance in men's shaving products over the past century. The company began in 1895 with the concept of a disposable razor blade developed by a salesman named King Gillette, who lived in Brookline, Massachusetts. After six frustrating years of seeking funding for his venture, he combined forces with an MIT engineer and redesigned the product into what became the safety razor, which took off like a rocket around the revolutionary concept of safe self-shaving. The appearance in every World War II soldier's kit of the Gillette razor further propelled this product as the global standard.

Over the next fifty years, Gillette stayed relatively close to its core, adding new forms of shavers, shaving creams, and women's products. The past few decades, however, have seen the company reach out in many directions for new adjacencies, as its core shaving franchise captured such high market share that much of its growth had to come from the introduction of more elaborate systems like the Sensor, rather than from unit growth. Over time, Gillette added Braun electrical appliances (1967), Oral-B toothbrushes (1984), Parker Pen writing instruments (1992), and Duracell batteries (1996).

Some were justified by their impact on noncore businesses, where the acquisition was perceived to generate leadership in a new core area (adding Parker Pens to Waterman). Some were justified by the hope of leveraging the customer acceptance and infrastructure of the core toiletry franchise (Right Guard for men, Toni for women). Still others were justified more traditionally by their impact on the core business of shaving. For instance, in 1967 Gillette acquired Braun's small appliance business to help Gillette distribute its products better in international markets and to add Braun's electric "dry-shaver" technology to the Gillette product line. Braun was a successful acquisition that strengthened the core shaving franchise. Under Gillette's ownership, Braun grew from $70 million of sales to more than $1.7 billion and is now the second largest profit contributor, next to wet-shaving products. Interestingly, the core wet-shaving business plus the direct defensive and offensive acquisitions strongly related to the core account for virtually all of Gillette's corporate profit and new growth today.

From 1994 until 2005, when P&G acquired Gillette for $57 billion, blades and razors were the company's primary source of revenues and profits—nearly a century after Gillette was founded. By contrast, during the time before the merger with P&G, Gillette divested many other products (including cosmetics and stationery) because they were underperforming or were not one of the company's core businesses. In August 2000 Gillette sold its "struggling stationery division" to Newell Rubbermaid Inc., saying, "Our resources will now be devoted to the three core businesses."[6]

Hewlett-Packard's Imaging and Printing business unit is, on its own, a sustained growth company that has leveraged a strong original core, built in the 1980s, into a profitable $29 billion business in 2008. Between 1984 and 2000, the real take-off period of the market for small printers, the business grew at an average annual rate of more than 32 percent. The past growth pattern and the future strategic road map of the business demonstrate the power of a strategy that leverages and continually strengthens its core to yield ever larger and more attractive adjacencies. Moreover, they show how a business with high market share can continue to grow by finding adjacencies.

The printing and imaging business had humble beginnings on some farmland in Boise, Idaho, when a manager in the computer peripherals business was given permission to develop a line of small, low-cost desktop printers using the Canon laser printing engine for one line (LaserJet) and the HP-developed new inkjet technology for the other (ThinkJet). With its combination of high resolution and low cost, this business took off during the 1980s, creating a strong core that persists today. (Its U.S. market share is 55 percent in inkjet technology, with the equivalent numbers for Europe not far behind. As a result, HP's market position is approximately three times the size of its nearest competitor's—a huge advantage in cost, logistics, coverage, and brand awareness.)

Hewlett-Packard has driven its growth through four types of adjacency expansion. The first, through the continual search for increasingly refined customer segments around which to tailor and focus its core product, is into new customer segments. One example is the large-format plotting business for architects. Leveraging its 72 percent market share in large-format printing, HP developed innovative inkjet technology that offered high resolution, high color fidelity, and color registration to graphic artists and quickly captured that market. Another customer segment is the home digital photographer, a segment growing more than 300 percent annually, for which the company has developed a printer with embedded software that allows smart media cards to be inserted directly into the printer, rather than requiring decoding by a personal computer attached to the printer.

The second type of adjacency expansion, driven by technology adjacency and well-defined key customer needs, is into related product categories. A series of such moves has expanded Hewlett-Packard's business definition from printing to digital imaging. For example, as the graphic arts processes became increasingly digital, the company successfully entered the scanner market to better serve the needs of the graphic artist segment. It is now the number one supplier for all scanner segments. HP later combined the scanning technology with printing to create all-in-one products (printer/scanner/fax) for the small office and multifunction printers (printer/copiers) for the office environment. These two new product categories have provided high relative growth in the past few years. Still another example is the entry into the digital camera business, an effort to provide customers with a completely integrated digital photography solution.

The third type of expansion, through the search for more and more consumables and follow-on products for the core product lines, is into a broader range of printer supplies. For instance, HP entered the branded paper market and attained a surprisingly high market share. One specific example is the company's line of specially treated glossy paper for use with home digital photography, which holds the number two market position and is growing rapidly with high margins. This "razor-blade" model has been central to the growth and profitability of all of the HP printers, especially the inkjet.

Finally, the fourth type of expansion, through reconceptualizing the printing and imaging marketplace in terms of the creating, printing, and publishing of all documents, is into other copying and print processes. This move broadens the company's market from a $30 billion universe to a potential $130 billion one that includes newspapers, books, corporate central copying, and a variety of services for the home. One example is Hewlett-Packard's initiative to place printers throughout the home, either connected directly to the Internet or in devices such as set-top boxes, allowing everything from tickets ordered online to stamps to maps to advertising brochures to print from a TV console. Another example is a venture with NewspaperDirect to enable the remote printing of newspapers at hotels, eliminating costly transportation and allowing visitors to get their local papers even when traveling on distant continents. While the "inner core" of this business will remain the small, low-cost printers in direct lineage from the original product launch in the 1980s, the outer bounds of the industry are being expanded and pursued in a classic way: obtaining growth and profits from the core creatively but without overreaching and weakening the core.

We have catalogued case studies of hundreds of seemingly promising adjacency expansions that did not work out as forecast in financial plans. Indeed, almost every business executive has experienced adjacency expansion gone wrong. Venturing from the core is inherently risky. Yet if you are not venturing, and occasionally failing, you probably are not sufficiently pushing the boundaries. As Collins and Porras observe in *Built to Last*, "In examining the history of the visionary companies we were struck by how often they made some of their best moves not by detailed strategic planning, but rather by experimentation, trial and error, opportunism, and—quite literally—accident . . . Opportunistic experimentation and purposeful accidents."[7] The authors go on to describe the expansions of Johnson & Johnson into baby powder, Marriott into airport services, and American Express into travel services, all unscripted successes.

The company that does not have an organized way to experiment (General Electric refers to its experiments as setting up "popcorn stands") cannot reap the benefits of such "purposeful accidents."

Our intent in this chapter is not to pretend that we can offer a one-size-fits-all solution for deciding where to expand. What we can do, however, is suggest some methods for examining adjacencies that will improve the odds of making better decisions as well as raise warning flags on the most dangerous shoals that historically have shipwrecked the most growth strategies.

Defining and Mapping Adjacencies

It seems obvious that the stronger and more dynamic a company's core business, the broader its range of add-on expansion opportunities. It follows less obviously, however, that those companies with the strongest cores, and hence the most to sacrifice in losing focus, also suffer the greatest temptation to become distracted; they're confronted by the second paradox of growth. Therefore, companies trying to spring new growth out of a slowdown or to select new growth initiatives without jeopardizing a strong core can benefit from methodically inventorying and mapping out their adjacent opportunities.

The content for an adjacency map should come first from the opinions of the management team and then from employees in direct contact with customers, from outside observers of the company and its markets, and from a study of the list of new businesses being funded by venture capitalists in related areas. Once at an executive conference, John Chambers of Cisco said that he carries around a card with the names of the twenty-five small company start-ups most relevant to his core businesses.

There are three basic types of adjacency expansion:

1. A direct move into an immediate opportunity. This is by far the largest category of adjacencies. One example is Enterprise Rent-A-Car (the leader in "replacement" rentals at body shops) acquiring Alamo Rent A Car and National

Car Rental in order to move aggressively into the airport rental car segment. Another is Starbuck's decision to expand its chain of stores into a new geography such as China. A third is eBay's extension of its online auction franchise from consumer products to business products, a customer segment adjacency. And everywhere we see local restaurants offering a home-delivery service or a takeout dinner menu, or setting up a small area in the restaurant for their signature foods—a simple product adjacency.

2. An "option" purchased in a business related to the core; a hedge against future uncertainties. Many of Intel's and Microsoft's venture investments and technology acquisitions could be considered hedges against or windows into future technology shifts.

3. A series of sequential moves that expand the boundaries and capabilities of the core business. A classic example of this would be the movement of some of the leading telecom companies with a legacy in wireline telephony—like KPN in the Netherlands or Telstra in Australia—into a range of services from fixed telecom to mobile telecom to ADSL (broadband) to VoIP/video calls/IPTV. This is consistent with technology convergence and customer interest in an integrated "single bill" offering in that industry. Another example would be Cisco's acquisition of Pure Digital Technologies in 2009 for $590 million in stock. Pure Digital gives Cisco additional technologies and know-how to enable it to move a step closer to visual networking and provide a broader offering to consumers for their "media-enabled" home.

Adjacency maps can reveal complexity of choice and trade-offs, as demonstrated by the map shown in figure 3-1. The choices are depicted as spokes leading out of the core business. One set of spokes and the branches off it might represent customer segments where

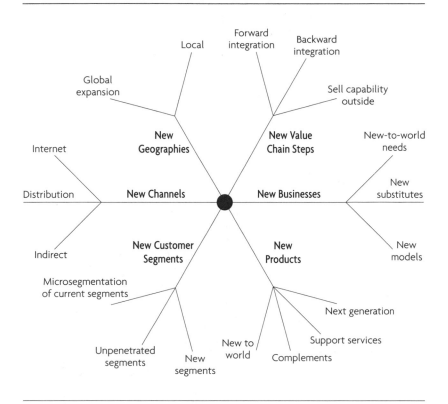

3-1 Adjacencies Radiate from the Core

expansion possibilities reside. A second might represent new channels, a third new geographic areas, a fourth changes to the value
chain, a fifth new businesses, and a sixth new products.

As another example, figure 3-2 shows a differently configured
adjacency map, this one specifically for a company in the alcoholic
beverages business. Along each spoke, opportunities radiate outward from the most- to the least-immediate extensions of the core
business. It is possible, for a given strategy, to rank on the spokes
those opportunities that are highest priority and those that are
marginal.

There are obviously many possible processes for mapping out
and characterizing the full range of business adjacencies. Here is

3-2 The Multistep Adjacency Map of an Alcoholic Beverages Company

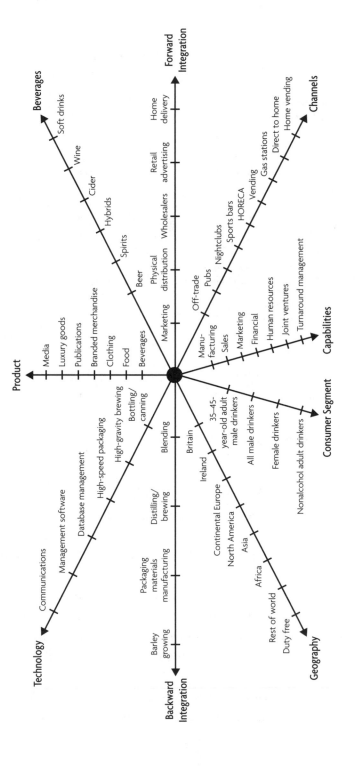

one that we have used productively. Begin by defining the core and gaining consensus about the most potent source of competitive differentiation and advantage. Having done that, identify and describe adjacencies step by step in the following order:

1. Identify the adjacencies you are in and array the data on how you are doing in each (market share, profitability, investment).

2. Identify the adjacencies your organization is considering or has rejected.

3. Identify other known adjacencies, including those that might require two or three strategic moves to reach.

4. Identify adjacencies suggested by your competitors' investment actions.

5. Identify adjacencies suggested by potential new competitors, often small companies.

6. Identify future adjacencies that may be created by technology or other developments.

7. Put all of these adjacencies onto a single grid or map (such as the maps shown in figures 3-1, 3-2, and 3-3), and push your thinking about what additional adjacencies might still be missing.

Having developed an inventory of adjacencies and growth opportunities surrounding the core, do a quick ranking and rating of each. Such a ranking might be based on the following types of qualitative and quantitative measures: potential size, strength of advantage due to uniqueness of the core, strength of probable competition, offensive and defensive importance to the core (warding off invaders), a long-term perspective on multistep moves, and ability to implement. Forcing a ranking almost always stimulates a highly productive management discussion of core strategic issues grounded in data.

Finally, develop clusters of moves, or strategic scenarios, and do the tough financial and analytic work of developing your growth strategy. None of these activities is easy, but all are essential (in some form) for most businesses to engage in periodically.

As mentioned earlier, we are often struck by how many companies—from complex divisions of large corporations to small, early stage companies—do not look at their growth opportunities at the same time, in a strategic context, with a fact base to help support the priorities. The Bain annual survey of tools and techniques, conducted across a sample of 475 companies, provides corroborating evidence. In 2000, this survey found that "growth strategies" were the sixth-most-used tool, along with other standards like "pay-for-performance" systems and "customer satisfaction assessments," among the best-performing companies. By contrast, growth strategies didn't appear in the top ten techniques of the worst-performing companies. In a way, these companies are like people who are lost and neither have maps with them nor value carrying maps at all. By 2006, the survey showed that the percentage of companies using tools of growth strategies had increased from 55 percent to 65 percent. In the 2009 survey, as the world economic crisis loomed, this dropped to 38 percent, showing a preoccupation with cost reduction even though, in the same survey, 53 percent of executives said that they felt that their companies were overemphasizing cost reduction initiatives relative to the promise of revenue and growth.

The process of mapping does more than just help organize opinions and inventory ideas. It reveals the extent to which the organization has a multiplicity of choices for growth and makes it easier to understand the trade-offs that may need to be made in choosing which to fund. In the absence of such a process, organizations often lack an agreed-on big-picture context for making decisions, fund an excessive number of initiatives to an insufficient extent, and take too seriously the "idea of the day."

Our experience and our review of sustained value creators show that a handful of most frequent adjacency expansion directions constitutes about 90 percent of the growth initiatives that are adjacent to a core business. The most common adjacencies to a core business are the following:

- Interlocking customer and product adjacencies
- Share-of-wallet adjacencies
- Capability adjacencies
- Network adjacencies
- New-to-the-world adjacencies

Interlocking Customer and Product Adjacencies

Perhaps the most common adjacency expansion is moving into new customer and product segments, using each move to reinforce the next. For some businesses, this approach to reinvesting has proven sufficient for decades of growth. It involves constantly adapting a product to enter a new customer segment and drawing on the knowledge gained about that customer segment to develop new product ideas that can then be applied in still other segments.

ServiceMaster has used this approach with great success. The company's origins trace to a 1930s mothproofing business run by Marion Wade, a former minor league baseball player who still dreamed of the big leagues. From there, it moved into carpet cleaning, riding the wave of postwar installation of wall-to-wall carpets throughout America. The company was named "ServiceMaster" in 1958 by Wade, a devout Christian who wanted to emphasize the importance of constantly serving the Master. The company's mission statement includes four commandments: (1) to honor God in all we do, (2) to help people develop, (3) to pursue excellence, and (4) to grow profitably.

Over the forty years between the late 1950s and late 1990s, ServiceMaster executed on these objectives to grow by a compound annual rate of 21 percent and consistently earned a return on equity of more than 20 percent. In the 1990s, it provided its investors an average annual return of more than 34 percent.

ServiceMaster's growth strategy has followed a consistent formula for over half a century, moving from one product segment into an adjacent product, then into a closely related customer segment, and so on. This growth is shown in figure 3-3 as a series of concentric rings representing growth into adjacent areas over successive periods of time. You can see the business expanding out from carpet cleaning to cleaning in general for residential and commercial businesses. General cleaning led the company in the 1960s to start cleaning hospitals (a suggestion made by a nun to the religious founder), where it also developed a grounds-management business. This new service then was sold to ServiceMaster's original segments of residential and commercial customers. Cleaning naturally led to laundry services. Grounds management led to pest control. This set of services led to a strategy to serve educational institutions. And so on, step by step, decade after decade.

ServiceMaster's growth has been more than 75 percent organic. However, the company has used acquisitions strategically to bring in new products and capabilities that are fully "plug compatible" with its core customers and that serve as catalysts for new growth. For example, in 1986, it acquired Terminix, the second-largest pest control agency in the United States, and leveraged its core customer base to achieve leadership in the new sector. In 1989, ServiceMaster acquired Merry Maids, a franchiser of professional maid services, which is now the leader in its business. In the 1990s, it purchased two lawn care operations, TruGreen and ChemLawn, which it consolidated and grew to create the leading lawn care business. Growth through pursuing close adjacencies, segment by segment, has proven a long-term formula for success for ServiceMaster.

A 1985 article about the company noted:

> A big numeral 2 rests on a cabinet in Pollard's [the president and CEO in 1985] office, under a wall full of co-workers' photos. It represents a goal of $2 billion in sales by 1990. Reminded that ServiceMaster hadn't reached $1 billion yet, and that its largest market recently got a lot tougher, Pollard replied with a grin, "Well, I like to make goals and beat 'em."[8]

3-3 ServiceMaster Expands Its Services and Customers More Than Fifty Years

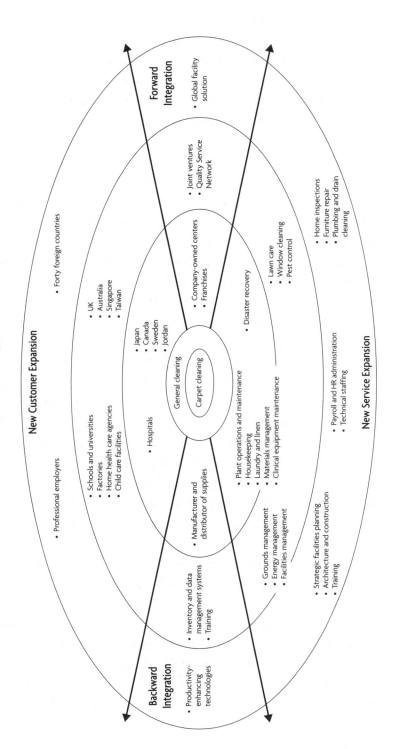

In 2007, ServiceMaster was purchased by the private equity firm Clayton Dubilier & Rice, the year after it was named as one of "America's Most Admired Companies" by *Fortune* magazine.

De Beers is an example of a company that created growth for itself by helping its direct customers, jewelers, find new adjacencies to penetrate around their core business. One way was by using its marketing prowess to inextricably link its products with important occasions. De Beers's marketing efforts almost single-handedly turned wearing a diamond engagement ring into a cultural imperative in Japan, for instance. De Beers began its campaign in 1966, when the diamond engagement ring acquisition rate for all brides in Japan was 6 percent. By 1998, that rate had grown to 65 percent.

After the diamond engagement ring market was firmly established worldwide, De Beers reached out to a slightly older segment of women in a different geographic area with its promotion of the diamond anniversary band. From 1988 to 1999, the diamond anniversary band acquisition rate in the United States for all women on their tenth anniversary soared from 3 percent to 16 percent.

De Beers used the millennium to its advantage. The company invested heavily in advertising, suggesting that the ultimate gift for the new millennium is a diamond. Sales in the first half of 2000 were up by 44 percent over the same period in 1999 due, in large part, to this initiative. In addition, De Beers shifted its focus to the diamond solitaire necklace in the United States, increasing sales from around $375 million in 1996 to $750 million in 1998. It also heavily promoted diamond ear studs in Japan, with equally dramatic results.

But it is interesting to see how things change and how adjacent moves from the core often take on larger significance than simply providing new sources of growth. In 2000, De Beers encountered a true crisis in its original supply-driven core. The company that had mined more than 90 percent of the diamonds in the world for more than a century saw its competitive advantage erode as the global market for diamonds turned to negative rates of growth and De Beers' market share slipped to around 45 percent. However, the company had hidden assets to rebuild its strategy: its customer relationships, the power of its brand, and its experience with customer desires and buying patterns. De Beers recovered rapidly because of these assets and this adjacency experience. As Gareth Penny, the group managing director, explained:

> It was clear when the senior team got together in 1999 that we had to make major changes. You have to start with the big questions: What is your DNA? What is it you are really good at? I think most people are not very good at understanding their core . . . We have been more successful than we expected. Driving demand, we have gone from negative growth in diamond jewelry worldwide to more than 3 percent growth per annum and, more recently, to more than 5 percent growth. This is a significant accomplishment in a $60 billion global industry. By 2001, we valued the diamond part of the business at $9.3 billion, quite a change from its estimated value of only $1 billion just two years earlier."[9]

Share-of-Wallet Adjacencies

A second strategy for growing beyond the initial boundaries of a core business is through moving into "share-of-wallet" adjacencies. By capturing most of the purchases your core customers make and then expanding their menu for purchases, it is possible to create a bond with your customers that substantially increases their loyalty. Such loyalty in the core customer base has several self-reinforcing economic consequences for strategy. First, it allows the cost of serving a customer to be spread across more purchases. Second, it increases both the retention rate and the life-cycle value of a customer. Third, it provides an opportunity to establish a deeper relationship with a customer, a by-product of which is more intimate knowledge of each other's businesses. Finally, it serves as a competitive deterrent, dramatically increasing switching costs. In some situations, doubling share of wallet can create a three- to four-times increase in profitability.

One of the clearest proofs of the lasting success of a share-of-wallet strategy is the Walt Disney Company's track record in expanding adjacencies from its core business with its deep roots in animated cartoons. The company began in 1923 as a partnership to develop animated cartoons. Its first product was a series of *Steamboat Willie* cartoons. In even this formative period of the company, the core of imaginative characters and application of the newest technical effect or innovation is apparent. *Steamboat Willie*, set to the music of "Turkey in the Straw," was the first cartoon to include synchronized sound. The most successful Disney products more than seventy years later, such as *Fantasia 2000*, remained strikingly similar. *Toy Story*, *Toy Story 2*, and *Dinosaur*, for example, were the first box-office hits to use computer animation throughout. Innovation punctuates the history of the Disney core, from the first full-color production to the first full-length animation, *Snow White and the Seven Dwarfs*, to the first integrated film and animation product, *Who Killed Roger Rabbit?*

In the early years, Disney's promotional skills and ability to find product adjacencies surrounding the core also became evident with the introduction of Mickey Mouse school writing tablets in 1929:

> These writing tablets were the beginning of the cross-promotion of Disney's cartoon characters that eventually made Walt Disney Productions a model of what business schools would later call "synergy" . . . Within three years, Ingersoll-Waterbury Co. was selling more than a million Mickey Mouse watches annually. Within a decade, ten percent of the company's revenues came from the royalties derived from the licensing of cartoon characters.[10]

Expanding these core assets, Disney marched into the construction of Disneyland in 1955 and into television with the companion *Disneyland* and *Mickey Mouse Club* shows. Each adjacency begot more related adjacencies. Disneyland sired Walt Disney World and Epcot Center. The early licensing efforts parented a series of generations of now-familiar Disney products such as books, records, plush characters, and magazines. These, in turn, spawned the chain of Disney Stores in 1987 and the hugely successful Disney Home Video business that same year. Not all of Disney's expansions worked. One restaurant initiative called Mickey's Kitchen was tried and abandoned. But the company was quick to experiment, and quick to stop the losers and fund every aspect of the winners. Over time, the box-office attendance of *Lion King*, for example, accounted for less than 20 percent of total profits from the film, with most of the profit pool shifting into new adjacencies from videos to retail products to Broadway adaptations. Though this strategy was executed a number of years ago, it remains one of the most vivid examples of rejuvenating a core through a repeatable formula of adjacency expansion.

Certainly, all has not been easy in the magic kingdom. Along the way there have been major crises of leadership and family succession, problems of cost overruns on projects such as Epcot, and problems of being slow to adapt to the changing tastes of an increasingly sophisticated child and teenage marketplace. Disney began to yield to the dangerous temptation to invest in departures from the core. Desperately seeking a way to find the next large wave of growth, Disney acquired sports teams (Anaheim Angels and Mighty Ducks), media companies (Capital Cities/ABC), real estate ventures (time-sharing businesses), and magazine properties (Fairchild Publications). During this acquisition period, Disney stock languished and investors, as is so often the case after the fact, called for a return to core growth.

More recently, the company has pursued joint ventures that leverage the original core, such as its agreement with NTT DoCoMo to make the rich content of Disney available over the Internet in Japan in a variety of wireless environments, and related acquisitions such as the computer animation specialist Pixar. Today, these core-driven initiatives look promising, and Disney has divested a range of noncore assets, stating, "We are not a conglomerate. If there are things that are maybe just off the core that we could monetize in a very strong economy, we may do that."[11]

The lessons from Disney are these. First, the original core can remain a source of adjacency growth for decades, if not longer, if managed properly and with adjacencies constantly monitored and assessed. Second, even the strongest core needs to be adapted in keeping with changes in its customer needs and technologies. Finally, even the most focused, excellent companies can choose adjacent moves that they later regret, only to return to the core.

Consider yet another share-of-wallet example. The Boots Company is one of the United Kingdom's largest retail chains, with a brand name more trusted than the Royal Family, according to one source. Founded as an herbal remedy shop for the poor in 1849, it has lived a history of growth almost continually for more than 150 years, expanding into adjacencies of its original core medicinal dispensary. In 1989, in an aggressive move to obtain a higher share of its customers' wallets, it acquired Payless DIY and WH Smith's Do It All, merging these businesses to access the home do-it-yourself business.

As readers of this book might now expect, nine painful years and more than $600 million of investments later, Boots sold its DIY chain at a large loss and returned to its core. A Boots spokesman commented, "Our strategy has to be to differentiate the brand—we are not a health and beauty supermarket, we are a health and beauty expert."[12] Developing closer-in adjacencies in niche, health-related, higher-margin products and customer segments is now the more modest, and more profitable, goal. In 2006 Boots combined with Alliance Unichem and rebranded the nine hundred Alliance stores as Boots in a merger executed by the private equity firm KKR. Today, it enters a new phase with supermarket competitors like Asda (owned by Wal-Mart) and Tesco, the leading grocery chain in the United Kingdom (with successful prescription services in many of its large, low-cost stores). Boots is responding by moving into higher-growth and potentially higher-value adjacencies including health and wellness, product innovation, and investments in customer loyalty. But virtually all observers of the company agree that "the nation's chemist" lost considerable momentum and squandered resources by its misconceived adjacency move years earlier.

With the amount of recent business analysis on the drivers of customer profitability and loyalty, the term *share of wallet* has moved into the common business lexicon. American Express has built the foundation of its card-member strategy on adding services and increasing card flexibility to increase the share of wallet of its most profitable customer segments. Dell tracks its share of wallet for computer-related purchases of key segments and customers. The celebrated USAA business model is built on tracking a customer through his or her life cycle, aiming at maximizing the company's share of wallet at each stage. Industrial companies such as PPG Industries have developed programs around the full life-cycle use of their automotive coating products from priming to painting to cleanup to color-matching technologies for repairs of scratches. It bundles and sells products and services as integrated systems. The idea that new market share in the best customers is the most valuable of all is probably as old as business itself. What is new are our deeper understanding of the economic magnitude of share of wallet and our more sophisticated techniques for tracking and driving growth through share of wallet.

Capability Adjacencies

Capability adjacencies are moves outward from the core that are based on deep organizational know-how. In our sustained value creator companies, we have identified three forms of capability-based expansions. The first is grounded in technology or technical know-how. The second comes from business process know-how and the management model for running businesses. The third is founded on knowledge about how to store, manage, and obtain value from information, and the peculiar economics of doing so.

Motorola is one of the pioneers of wireless communications and technology and a great business-growth story of the end of the twentieth century. Though the company is currently addressing a slowdown in its growth rate, its longer-term record is exceptional. In 1979, Motorola was a $2.7 billion company with earnings of $154 million and market value of $1.6 billion. By 1995, the company had grown revenues ten times, earnings twelve times, and market value twenty-three times. Motorola's growth, which illustrates the first type of capability adjacency, derives from its deep skills in engineering wireless systems. Deep knowledge of wireless engineering, constantly refined, formed the backbone of Motorola for more than seventy years. Businesses where wireless system capability was not key to competitive advantage (such as automobile heaters) or where this capability conveyed declining competitive advantage (such as consumer televisions) were also those businesses where profitable growth was difficult to achieve or altogether nonexistent.

Motorola began in 1928 when the Galvin brothers, Paul and Joseph, purchased a battery eliminator business out of bankruptcy. Battery eliminators are devices that allowed early battery-powered radios to run on household current. This business quickly led the company into radios for consumer automobiles and police cruisers, a market that it dominated. During World War II, Motorola developed and produced the field radios, "walkie-talkies," that virtually became a symbol of the war and led to the firm's first public stock offering in 1943. During its growth, the company experimented with business adjacencies ranging from eight-track tape players to push-button gasoline car heaters, both of which failed. At the withdrawal of the heater product Paul Galvin announced: "We will now stick to electronics." Not a bad choice.

The adjacency expansion path of Motorola started in 1928 from the first battery eliminator. Since then, the company has built on its core wireless-engineering knowledge in essentially all of its successful adjacency expansions, including its forays into home radios, pagers, cellular phones, and the infrastructure for cellular phone systems. The success predictors of its expansions were the extent to which the core wireless technology was critical to the business and the extent to which market power and influence could be built on that technology. In 1969, Neil Armstrong's first communication from the moon was sent via a Motorola transponder—a symbol of the "core of the core" of the ultimate engineering company.

Sadly, the leadership position in wireless handsets that Motorola had built has now eroded significantly. Strategic focus, or its absence, is at the center of this in a variety of ways. During the crucial investment period when many players jockeyed for a competitive position in the handset market, Motorola made its major corporate investment initiative in a project called Iridium. Iridium was a massive adjacency expansion for Motorola. Costing more than $6 billion, it consisted of a constellation of sixty-six low-Earth-orbiting satellites that would create a global cellular network. Not only was the project a failure, ending in bankruptcy, but it was a distraction of talent, attention, and capital. At the same time, Nokia got more focused, developing the elements of its repeatable formula in the handset market. By 2009, Nokia had captured an amazing 40 percent of all global mobile handsets, while Motorola stood behind Samsung in fourth position with a 6 percent market share. It probably did not have to be this way. Perhaps Iridium was a logical adjacency for Motorola to pursue, but to allow it to consume the amount of capital and attention that it did (versus other structures to gain an "option value" but insulate the core better) proved to be a costly decision.[13]

In their seminal article on core competence, C. K. Prahalad and Gary Hamel assert that many companies' growth strategies will "be judged on their ability to identify, cultivate, and exploit the core competencies that make growth possible—indeed, they'll have to rethink the concept of the corporation itself."[14] Prahalad and Hamel elaborate particularly on the examples of NEC and 3M, explaining that these companies have a strategic architecture that makes their competencies transparent and relevant in many settings. The case of Motorola, described above, illustrates an extreme example of a company whose profitable growth is a function of how it manages a relatively tightly defined set of capabilities into new business opportunities that surround the core. The tension lies between protecting the core (while not creating a static state) on the one hand and expanding into the right adjacencies (without abandoning the core) on the other.

Network Adjacencies

Robert Metcalfe, the developer of Ethernet technology and a student of networks, has observed that the power of an interconnected network rises geometrically with the number of users. The economics of networks in which the addition of a user increases the value of the network to all other users gives rise to increasing returns to scale and therefore to large rewards for network-dependent businesses that expand. Increasing returns create situations where incremental scale can be worth more to the leader than to other participants. This is why many software and communications businesses have characteristics of natural monopolies. Growth through incremental network expansion is valuable indeed for such companies. Economists have studied the competitive dynamics of networks extensively.[15]

For our purposes, many types of network adjacencies provide attractive growth opportunities for companies whose economics hinge on network effects. Perhaps the most obvious type is adding adjacent networks to a distribution or communications network. Consolidation of the railroads and, more recently, consolidation of cellular networks demonstrate this type of adjacency expansion, as does Vodafone's takeover of AirTouch in the United States and of Mannesmann in Germany.

Another type is accumulating groups of customers who can be put on a common information platform or service. Becoming the accepted standard for a consumer or business application software is of immense value. The growth strategies of Microsoft Office in desktop software, eBay in online auctions, SAP in business system software, Google in online search, and even Facebook in social networking all build on the power of becoming the standard in their "core of the core" combined with the network economics that are attendant on this position in many software and online businesses.

New-to-the-World Adjacencies

Just as volcanic disturbance can send new, and therefore uninhabited, land up from the ocean, so, too, can industry turbulence create new, uninhabited business territory. Often this territory comprises new-to-the-world businesses, and it can represent an important, opportunistic form of adjacency expansion. We have found two main ways that such adjacencies emerge, become recognized, and are pursued successfully.

The first is where a leading-edge business in a relatively dynamic market determines that it has built world-class capabilities in an area where others—not necessarily competitors—wish to purchase that know-how for their own business purposes. For example, Cisco, one of our sustained value creators, found that many of its customers were asking whether it would be willing and able to transfer some of its business practices, especially those related to the use of the Internet and information technology, to help them transform their internal processes and become more efficient. Cisco has discovered that this consulting capability is not only valuable in itself as a business, but it can strengthen the company's core hardware business. Amazon, the online retailer, developed sophisticated algorithms to customize its webpage to each user using his or her underlying behavioral data from purchases and click-through. This capability has become an enormous competitive advantage in selling information products, but is now also a separate business where Amazon will assist with, or take over, online retailing for noncompetitive partners. Similarly, Google has made a business out of its knowledge of tailoring its search software to specific applications called Google Search Solutions for Business.

The second primary way that such new-to-world adjacencies emerge is through a major change in consumer behavior—either the emergence of a new subsegment of consumers or new behaviors from an existing segment—often enabled by new technology. For instance, the Geek Squad (a service adjacency of more than 24,000 employees that helps consumers install and use digital products—like Internet networks, PC security software, and home entertainment systems) filled an enormous consumer need in dealing with an ever more sophisticated array of equipment and software. Perhaps some of the iPod adjacencies by Apple such as the AppStore (for downloading applications) or iTunes (for downloading music and songs) were clearly "white space adjacencies" enabled by new consumer behavior and new technology.

Evaluating Adjacency Expansion Opportunities

Management teams that develop a full inventory of growth opportunities and adjacency expansions around their core business(es) quickly recognize that they are awash in interesting and potentially attractive options for investment. Before they undertake a major data collection effort, they should step back and apply their strategic judgment and operating knowledge of the business to rate the opportunities along five key dimensions:

1. How much does this strengthen, protect, and reinforce the core?

2. What are the chances of our becoming a leader in the new segment or business?

3. Could this move have a defensive benefit, preempting or interdicting our present or future competitors?

4. Does this investment position our core business strategically for an even stronger future set of adjacency moves, such as hedging against a major uncertainty or constituting one step in a well-defined sequence of strategic moves?

5. Can we be certain of superbly executing implementation?

We find that these questions provoke a rich and active discussion of priorities and lead to a second phase of prioritization of the activities that rate best. In general, if an opportunity fails on two dimensions, substantial questions should be raised about its attractiveness.

This second phase of prioritization can be more traditional and analytic, building a fact base on the following criteria:

- The size of the opportunity; that is, the current and future profit pool

- The strength of competitive activity

- Evidence about customer value and demand

- The magnitude and timing of investment

- The magnitude and timing of potential revenues and costs

- Uncertainties that could magnify or shrink the opportunity

- Difficulty rating of implementation

The final phase of ranking and selecting involves clustering the investment initiatives into distinct strategic scenarios. In one industrial company typical of many we have seen, the alternatives clustered into two scenarios. One option was built around a long list of initiatives for rejuvenating growth in a profitable but static core business. The initiatives included expanding internationally, forming smaller units for small customers, creating value-added services, providing information products, and developing new technology products. A second option entailed building mass and focus around several emerging customer segments. What began as an adjacency mapping exercise with more than ninety different ideas evolved into a highly productive strategic discussion about the future course of the business and where to deploy key financial, scientific, and management resources.

The logic for choosing a direction for growth is also changing. Industry turbulence is both increasing the amount of uncertainty surrounding many choices and shortening the time frame for reaction. In addition, growth choices that were once primarily clustered in concentric circles around a core business (product choices, customer segment choices, geographic sequencing decisions) now include a much more vexing and fundamental set of adjacent opportunities (totally new businesses, hedging).

Furthermore, the cycle time of strategy development is becoming shorter and shorter in many industries. As a result, the evaluation exercise described, which once might have been conducted annually (or less frequently) over a several-day period, now needs to be accelerated to quarterly, monthly, or weekly and compressed to a day.

Multiple-Move Adjacencies and Options

We argue throughout this book that industry structures are becoming less stable, leadership is becoming more fleeting, and the life span of a typical strategy is growing shorter. Risk and uncertainty loom increasingly larger in business life. In an environment like this, adjacency expansions are critical for staking your claim on future market positions as a hedge against uncertainty. The case for making these investments can sometimes be enhanced by going beyond basic net present value calculations and gut instinct to call on frameworks from options theory.[16]

Many examples exist of adjacency moves that hedged against an uncertain future successfully. The investment that Roche made in the biotech company Genentech put it out ahead of its "big pharma" rivals in this emerging area of science and led to subsequent adjacency moves such as Roche's acquisition of Cetus and of Boehringer Mannheim (a diagnostics company). These investments, in turn, put Roche in a position to become the leader in the new area of pharmacogenomics (genetic testing and molecular diagnostics).

The lesson from this, and from a proliferating number of similar examples, is that adjacency expansions can and should hedge against future uncertainties and foster learning, as well as attack existing pools of nearby profit. Both moves are critical building blocks for a sustainable growth strategy.

Adjacencies and Choice of Core

The combination of a rich set of adjacencies and a strong or dominant core business can be a powerful breeder reactor for creating sustained, profitable growth if accompanied by appropriately aggressive reinvestment. Businesses with rich adjacencies around a weak core must first identify or create a strong core around which to build. Businesses with strong leadership but few logical adjacencies may need to redefine parts of their core (as discussed in chapter 4). More common are companies with multiple businesses, all funded in similar ways through the budgeting process yet all with different underlying positions and adjacency potential. In this situation, the richness of adjacencies around competing cores can be the deciding factor in determining how and where to focus a company and drive higher levels of growth.

Common Pitfalls of Adjacency Expansion

Investment in adjacencies is eventually necessary for any company to continue creating value. It is also one of the riskiest activities a firm can undertake. In examining more than one hundred cases of business adjacency expansion, we have found seven primary pitfalls, or risk factors.

Pitfall 1: Expanding toward an Entrenched Position

Strategy, Liddell Hart's history of military strategy, examines the successes and failures of military campaigns to take over territory going back to the Peloponnesian Wars. Hart finds that armies that make a frontal assault on an entrenched position lose virtually 100 percent of the time, even with superior forces. He argues that an indirect approach is essential to increasing the odds of victory. For instance, Alexander's most decisive battle against the Persians, at Guagarela, was a masterful use of an indirect attack. In this battle, Alexander took a small fraction of his troops eighteen miles away from the front, attacking at an unexpected time from an unexpected direction while the majority of his troops were visible and immobile in the opposite direction. Alexander achieved an enormous psychological victory in addition to his military triumph. John Keegan writes that Alexander was "both outnumbered and irremediably overlapped, he had to devise a more subtle means to win victory." The indirect tactics he used "anticipated by 2,000 years the tactics that would make Frederick the Great the most celebrated soldier of his time." When the battle was over, Alexander had won decisively and "had established his authority over the whole of the empire and was poised to march 'to the end of the earth.'"[17] An analogous situation can be seen in business adjacency expansion. Launching a direct assault on entrenched positions, without a major new angle of attack or differentiation, seldom wins the war. Yet many companies try to move into adjacencies that are, in fact, the well-defended, entrenched positions of others.

One of Bain Capital's most successful investments was in Wesley-Jessen. Bain Capital acquired the contact lens manufacturer for $6.4 million and took it public four years later to the tune of $290 million in equity, nearly a fifty-times return. Bain saw a strong core (specialty lenses) underexploited because of a mistaken pattern of adjacency expansion. "W-J decided that it was going to move into the mass market for disposable contact lenses against Johnson & Johnson and Bausch & Lomb," explains Mitt Romney. "It built a $100 million factory to compete in this high-volume, low-cost segment and lost money every day doing that. In our opinion, W-J simply did not have the scale of the brand name to compete at the low end. This was a bad expansion strategy, too far from the core specialty segment where it was excellent. We saw this right away during due diligence. Our first action after the acquisition was to close the disposable plant and refocus on specialty."

Romney goes on: "The second phase was adopting a strategy that went back to the core. This had two elements. The first was what we called 'the forgotten doctor strategy,' to refocus on the most sophisticated fitters of lenses in segments like toric lenses for astigmatism. The second element was to take W-J's strong position in tinted and colored lenses and really drive this as a style product, with purple lenses targeted at U.S. teenagers, other colors targeted at the Japanese market, ultraviolet protection targeted at sports, and so on. This segmentation strategy building on the original core has been hugely successful in driving profitable growth."[18]

Pursuing areas of the market in which a company has relatively low odds of leadership or of building market power and influence can sap resources from the core and actually retard growth in the rest of the business.

Pitfall 2: Overestimating the Profit Pool

The odds of achieving success are much greater when growth goes after an expanding and deep industry profit pool rather than a shallow one. In their analysis of the Gucci example described earlier, Jim Gilbert and Orit Gadiesh write:

> Gucci's misstep highlights the problem with growth: the strategies businesses use to expand their top line often have the unintended consequence of eroding their bottom line. Gucci attempted to extend its brand to gain sales—a common growth strategy—but ended up alienating its most profitable customer segments and attracting new segments that were less profitable. It was left with a larger set of customers, but a much less attractive customer mix.[19]

Mapping out the current and future profit pool is essential in developing a growth strategy. The profit pool is a function of potential market size and customer value from undertaking an activity. It is also a function of industry structure: The pool in a segment in which one participant can gain market power and influence is much larger than the pool in a segment that has multiple equal players.

Pitfall 3: False Bundling

If you flip through a pile of annual reports, you are sure to encounter at least a couple of phrases like the following: "Our aim is to serve all of the needs of our key customers." "We want to be the one-stop shop for all of our customers' needs." In a few situations, this all-things-to-all-people approach might be appropriate. However, in general, phrases like these are warning signs of business boundaries that are too broad to be practical and that can lead to a dangerous overextension of resources.

One such example is the case of U.K.-based bookseller WH Smith. This highly recognizable book business, which caters to travelers, began in 1792 as a single new store near London and quickly expanded into newspaper distribution around London. Its bookstall expansion was fueled by the train traveler who needed not only newspapers but other goods for long trips on cold trains, including games, foot warmers, and even rugs. Today, WH Smith has more than $3.5 billion in sales, a large distribution business, and well over one thousand stores of different types, still heavily catering to travelers.

With its core under attack from competitors like Dillon's and Waterstone's, WH Smith concluded that its problem was narrow participation in a broad retail space. The company began to fill that space by adding new retail product lines such as toys, typewriters, music, do-it-yourself tools, and gifts through its bookstores. The result was lower sales per square foot; higher costs in the form of inventory, infrastructure, and systems; and a management team distracted from defending the imperiled core of selling printed matter.

After losing £195 million ($310 million) in 1996, the board brought in new management with a new strategy: Return to the original view of WH Smith's marketplace and business definition.

Over the next two years, management dropped noncore products that had been added to the line and divested noncore acquisitions such as The Wall (a U.S. music retailer) and a majority stake in the Virgin Our Price megastore chain. It then used the money from these sales to reinforce and expand the core within the original business boundaries. In 1998, WH Smith purchased 230 U.K. newsstands from rival distributor John Menzies and began distributing its core products via the Internet. WH Smith still faces battles in a tough industry, but its gun sights are at least trained on the right battleground. It has posted positive revenue and profit performance in recent years, especially in its airport and train station locations—a modern version of its original train-oriented newspaper distribution core of the 1800s.

Some of the most well-documented examples of failed adjacency expansion are traceable to invalid assumptions about the economics of bundling. Allegis, the combination of United Airlines, Sheraton Hotels and Resorts, and Hertz predicated on offering the consumer a total travel package with a "one-stop shop," certainly illustrates a gigantic investment based on false expectations about consumer behavior. Similarly, Sears, in purchasing Coldwell Banker, Allstate Insurance Group, and Dean Witter Financial Services Group in order to offer its customers an integrated bundle of financial products, failed to realize that its department store customers simply weren't interested in the offering.

Pitfall 4: Invaders from Unexpected Fronts

The discovery of new, uninhabited market territory frequently brings invaders from unexpected directions. Consider the following:

- Kodak's pursuit of the digital camera market encounters unfamiliar competitors Hewlett-Packard and Canon.

- Quaker Oats' attempt to expand Snapple beverages runs directly into new drink initiatives of Coca-Cola, with its unassailable distribution infrastructure.

- Anheuser-Busch moves into salty snacks through the acquisition of Eagle Snacks, leading to the quick discovery that Frito-Lay is a more powerful competitor in its core than had been initially contemplated.

- Xerox's entry into low-end copiers gets a surprise attack from Canon, an unconventional competitor the giant had underestimated.

Lacking familiarity with new competitors, companies tend to underestimate their strength, nature, and angle of attack. Instead, they need to x-ray every new competitor thoroughly to understand the world from that adversary's point of view, economics, and customers.

The exercise of mapping adjacencies requires not just taking an inside-out look at the market, but also taking an outside-in look at which companies might be amassing forces at your back. In an increasingly fast-moving and interdependent world, competitive blindsiding is becoming more common.

Pitfall 5: Failing to Consider All Adjacencies

The Massachusetts-based Polaroid Corporation was arguably one of America's first successful technology companies. Edwin Land retired from Polaroid second only to Thomas Edison in total lifetime scientific patents granted, a remarkable achievement. Yet, as the nature of film and imaging changed repeatedly, right up to today's digital imaging, the company remained fixed on instant (chemistry-based) photography. Polaroid failed to redraw its boundaries to account for the new, much broader, customer- and competitor-driven definition of imaging. Polaroid's business definition, instant photography, was driven by an internal point of view too narrow to lead to sustained, profitable growth. Its strategy based on this definition (and associated set of assets) was certainly not successful and, in 2001, the company filed for Chapter 11 bankruptcy. After coming out of bankruptcy and undergoing further travails, the company again filed for Chapter 11 in 2008.

Companies like Polaroid, with a single, extremely strong product, historical technology, or long heritage of success in a protected niche, are the most vulnerable to drawing their business boundaries and list of options too narrowly. In these environments there are especially strong organizational and budgetary forces that can restrict business definitions. Narrow boundaries keep "apparent" market shares high, a crowd-pleaser to employees and analysts alike. Narrow boundaries provide psychological comfort and anaesthetize budget reviews. And, most important of all, narrow boundaries wall out the hard choices that may loom ahead.

Pitfall 6: Missing a New Segment

Failing to trace or pursue a newly emerging customer segment near your core can have lasting consequences. Consider, for example the case of rental cars.

Founded in the 1950s, the leading rental car companies, Avis, Hertz, and National Car Rental, focused on serving the business traveler in the top one hundred airports in the United States. But the strategy issue for the rental car companies became more blurry as new segments sprung up and began to grow and take on a life of their own. The first new car rental segment to sprout was leisure travel. The second was the replacement rentals, serving drivers whose cars were in the shop for repair.

Alamo Rent A Car was founded by Florida entrepreneur Mike Eagan in 1974, serving four locations with a fleet of one thousand cars. Alamo's formula was different because it was targeting a different population, the leisure market, paying for cars out of its own pocket. Eagan's model included lower-cost locations outside the airport, advertising focused at leisure destination and origin sites, and a dedicated sales force directed at travel agents and key influencers. Off-airport rentals are anathema to many time-sensitive business travelers on day trips, but they are perfect for the price-conscious family on vacation. Within fifteen years, Alamo had captured a leading share in the leisure segment and had grown its fleet to more than 150,000 cars, nearly 75 percent the size of the Hertz, Avis, and National fleets, on average.

As Alamo developed the leisure market, another company, Enterprise, developed the replacement market. In the 1960s, Enterprise's founders, the Taylor family, saw an opportunity to provide rental vehicles for motorists whose personal cars were unavailable due to accidents or repairs. Just as Alamo built a sales force presence in travel agents, so Enterprise invested to build a sales force presence at key body shops, insurance adjuster centers, and automobile dealers. These longer-term, even lower-cost rental needs required a different business model from Alamo's and a different business model from Hertz's or Avis's in terms of the condition of the cars, the size and quality of the locations, and staffing. In 1980, Enterprise had just ten thousand cars. Today, it has more than seven hundred thousand vehicles and has captured more than 70 percent of the replacement market, which it defined, created, and then dominated. It is now the most profitable major rental car company in terms of margin and return on capital.

Should the traditional rental car companies have pursued the leisure market more broadly during its early years of development, or the replacement market, or both? Would that have weakened their core airport business and allowed traditional competitors to make inroads? Or would early entry into leisure and replacement have been the winning strategy? Would the diversion of capital to develop these new businesses have sapped resources from more productive uses? Or would it have allowed them to strengthen their core by building a leading position in a new coalescing segment? Interestingly, Enterprise's focus and singular success in the replacement business paid off in ways perhaps never envisioned by the company. In 2007, the company purchased the erstwhile Vanguard Car Rental, formed by the merger of Alamo (leader in leisure) and National (number three in the airport rentals market). Strategically, Enterprise is now doubly formidable, with a strong position in the replacement market funding an assault on the airport market—using its own Enterprise brand as well as the two more established acquired brands.

Pitfall 7: Single-mindedly Pursuing High-end Adjacencies

As Clayton Christensen has documented in *The Innovator's Dilemma*, in their pursuit of adjacency expansion, the strongest core businesses gravitate to the higher and higher ends of their markets, targeting more sophisticated products with higher margins that can support greater overhead. In the computer industry, for example, virtually every manufacturer of components and PCs has a growth plan skewed toward more sophisticated new applications or toward selling a larger and larger percentage of new products to the large corporate data centers.

The danger is that this approach may expose a flank at the low end to attack from new breeds of low-cost competitors. Examples of successful attacks in such situations abound, in industries from steel (Nucor) to brokerage (Schwab online) to PCs (Dell) to rental cars (Enterprise) to airlines (Jet Blue) to investment funds (Vanguard). In selecting any growth strategy that expands into adjacencies, a company should ask itself whether it has avoided or inadequately defended against new competitors entering through the low-cost end of the market, and if so, why.

Containing the Risk of Dangerous Adjacencies: Diagnostic Questions

Clearly, the wrong choice or treatment of an adjacency expansion can do more than just lose money on that initiative; it can also distract core strategy, preoccupy management, and confuse investors with a multiplier effect to the detriment of all. There is no single formula for eliminating this risk. Indeed, bounded experimentation is at the head of the growth strategies of many of the companies that seem to expand rapidly from adjacency to adjacency.

In evaluating growth adjacencies, we have found a series of questions most useful in raising the right issues and, sometimes, clarifying the right answer. We recognize that many adjacencies fall into the close call area, especially where the future course of the marketplace is uncertain. However, even for those adjacencies, these questions can help to illuminate the nature of the risk and increase the possibility of lower-cost or lower-risk options.

To evaluate an adjacency investment, ask:

1. Does this adjacency strengthen or reinforce the core (or a core, if multiple cores exist)?

2. Does this adjacency add value for our core customers?

3. Does this adjacency serve as insulation against potential competitors' intent on attacking the core?

4. Is this adjacency positioned in the direction that the industry profit pool (and the core) is likely to shift over time (growing segments, channels, needed capabilities)?

5. Do we have a chance of achieving leadership economics in this adjacency through outright leadership, a protected customer position, or shared economics with the original core?

6. Does this adjacency hedge against a major strategic uncertainty?

7. Does this adjacency lead to other successive moves that, in total, are essential to build or protect the core?

8. Does this adjacency move into the backyard of a new competitor? What might the competitor's response be, and how does that play out?

9. Does failure to move into this adjacency turn out to render the core vulnerable several moves down the road? To what degree?

10. Have we fully mapped out all the competing adjacencies, or are we acting opportunistically, without fully calibrating the options?

Few adjacencies will win uniform endorsement from the answers to all ten questions. If you have an answer to or a point of view about each question and their sum total encourages you to move ahead, then you should probably pursue that adjacency. However, if you have developed no answer to or point of view about some of these questions, then you need to probe more deeply. The riskier the decision, the greater the need to consider alternative strategies, such as participating in minority positions or alliances in order to hedge the risk.

To evaluate the method chosen, ask:

1. If achieving leadership would be difficult, does it make sense to enter this adjacency by ownership rather than outsourcing or partnership?

2. If uncertainty is massive, do the adjacencies that most hedge against the future require majority ownership, or is it possible to have several minority vehicles with options to buy later?

3. If the new territory is unfamiliar, what experiments or pilots could be run? Do those signal competitive intent and provoke response?

4. Who is the current leader in the adjacency? Does it make more sense to combine forces in some fashion than to add a new competitor to the arena?

Conclusion

The most successful sustained growth companies almost always follow the pattern of expanding in a regular and organized way into a series of adjacencies around one or two strong cores. The pattern resembles the growth rings of a tree, emanating out from the center, expanding and reinforcing the core.

Determining which adjacencies to pursue and how much to invest in them relative to the core ranks at the top of difficult and seminal decisions for any company in its quest for sustained growth. We have examined case after case of how management teams have overreached, undervaluing their core in pursuit of far-reaching adjacencies (Bausch & Lomb). We have seen examples of companies that have tentatively moved into important adjacencies, only to provide them too little management talent and too few financial resources. Often, these companies further endangered the core while pursuing less relevant business initiatives at the same time (Polaroid). We have also looked at examples of companies that have been able to trigger wave after wave of new growth through an organized approach to resolving the tension between investing in the core and moving aggressively into adjacencies (the Hewlett-Packard printer business). Finally, we have seen cases of businesses that briefly departed from the core but that rushed back to reformulate the adjacency strategy in line with their true differentiation and turbocharged growth (Hilti).

Sophisticated management teams at the helms of all of these companies grappled mightily with the tension inherent in deciding whether to reinvest in the core, invest in adjacencies around the core, or consider hot new ideas that are distinct but that can build on strengths in the core. As their stories show, no one can bat one thousand. However, we hope that the examples, methods for mapping adjacencies, and diagnostic questions in this book will provide a useful framework for thinking about how to expand into the right adjacencies in the right way to gain full profit potential from the core.

The most successful companies have the largest number of new adjacencies raining down upon them every day. Success multiplies opportunities. Proliferating opportunities complicate decision making and prioritization (a good problem to have) and therefore risk. Paradoxically, the better your performance, the greater the risk in your decisions to select and invest in adjacencies around the core.

Of course, sometimes, the core itself encounters turbulence as technology changes or customer needs shift or a new business model appears on the horizon, gobbling up share in a surprising way. These situations are becoming increasingly common. Hence, we turn to our third element of growth strategy, redefining the core.

4

The Redefinition Dilemma

When naturalist Charles Darwin wrote of life on the Galapagos Islands in 1842, he noted an unusual strain of finch that had adapted to its environment to survive, and now looked and acted very differently from its continental cousins. These birds had elongated beaks that enabled them to eat local foods (insects, nuts, nectar from tropical fruits) that European finches didn't encounter. The evidence that a species had essentially redefined itself to successfully compete in a new environment became the cornerstone of Darwin's theory of evolution.[1] In the world of business, a similar evolution is taking place. Out of the turbulence in today's world, new environmental conditions are emerging, forcing companies to redefine themselves faster and more often than before in order to survive.[2]

To understand the magnitude and implications of industry turbulence, we did a simple comparison of more than forty major industry categories (airlines would be one, for example). For each, we defined turbulence in terms of major structural changes that would require companies to change the way in which they compete, and the way in which the profit pool is distributed. We did this comparison between the 1970s and the decade starting in 2000. We concluded that the rate of fundamental, structural turbulence is three times higher than it was a few decades ago—and that's not including the financial crisis of 2008–2009. In the 1970s only 15 percent to 25 percent of industries could be deemed turbulent by our definition; now the percentage ranges from 65 percent to 75 percent. Furthermore, in a subsequent analysis, we found that more than half of the profitability in the world (the world profit pool) was concentrated in six major industries—media, energy, airlines, financial services, telecommunications, and automotives—all of which could be classified as turbulent.

Our analysis identified five main types of forces that drive industry turbulence—allowing, in effect, for the creation of a scorecard for different levels of discontinuity. The first of these forces is a major change in regulation such as the deregulation of the airline industry decades ago, or the 2009 re-regulation of the banking sector. A second force of turbulence is the emergence of a "disruptive technology" that fundamentally changes industry economics and the rules of the game. A classic example is the effect of the emergence of digital photography on companies like Kodak and Polaroid—shifting the profit pool and redefining the winners. A third force, sometimes enabled by new technology, is the appearance of a fundamentally new-to-world business model with superior performance and economics to that of the past. The way that Dell took over the PC industry during the 1990s with its direct model is such an example. Before Dell, the concept of selling computers by phone or online direct to customers was unheard of, as was the lean inventory pipeline that supported the low-cost fulfillment of those orders. The emergence of low-cost carriers in the airline industry such as Jet Blue is another. The fourth force that can destabilize winners and losers and drain the profit pools is a radical change in consumer behavior patterns, sometimes accelerated by technology. So, for example, the demise of traditional newspapers, or the erosion of retail bookstores is driven by a dramatic shift in how younger people obtain information. Finally, there's the effect of developing economies—especially China and India—which have impacted manufacturing industry cost structures, as well as commodity prices, so profoundly. Many industries such as newspapers, or financial services, or media are feeling several of these forces at the same time.

The power of industry turbulence in determining winners and losers is apparent from an analysis we did of the sustained value creators during the 1990s with the companies creating market value at the fastest rate in the last three years of that decade (not sustained value, necessarily, but created value). To examine this, we categorized the sustained value creators according to whether their primary growth engine was the historic core performance and adjacency expansion (such as UPS or Wal-Mart), a new-to-the-world business model or market (such as eBay or Dell), or a true transformation of a historic core (such as Schwab or Nokia). Then we applied the same categories to the best-performing large companies. The comparison is shown in figure 4-1. Companies during that decade grew and prospered primarily through core growth and adjacency expansion. In fact, 84 percent followed this traditional

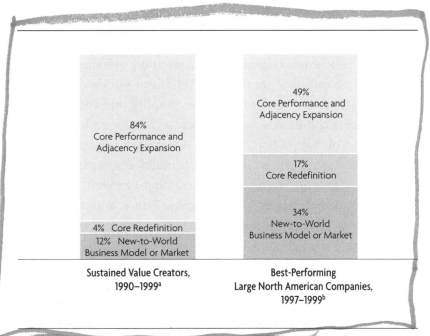

4-1 Turbulence Is Changing the Sources of Growth

a. Based on sample of U.S. sustained value creators; n = 67.

b. Large companies with highest three-year rate of value creation (through 12/31/99) as reported in the *Wall Street Journal*; n = 35.

pattern. By contrast, companies that achieved the highest levels of performance from 1997 to 2000 were those that took advantage of turbulence to drive into a major new-to-the-world market, develop a totally new business model, or radically transform their core more rapidly than adjacency expansion would allow. More than half of the best performers in that latter group were focused on new markets or forged from core redefinitions.

These studies were performed a decade ago, but recent analyses confirm that their conclusions are still valid today. For instance, a study of the thirty-three fastest-growing companies in eight countries from 1987 to 2007 revealed that a staggering two-thirds of them were new companies with a new-to-world business model. Moreover, 36 percent of these new companies created a previously nonexistent profit pool.

The Rarity of Successful Transformation

The need to redefine a core business fundamentally is becoming more critical and will become more common given the increasing frequency of industry turbulence. Yet history shows successful transformation to be quite rare. In examining our 240 sustained value creating companies' histories over a decade, we found fewer than thirty companies that arguably underwent a major redefinition of their core business. We then conducted a search of other studies of successful business transformation of major companies in the past decade, scanned the business press, and reexamined our own archives. Even expanding the universe in this way to some two thousand companies, we found fewer than one hundred that transformed their cores fundamentally (with scale more than $500 million). Indeed, in our literature search, about fifteen common examples constituted most of the mentions of transformation. The most frequently cited of these companies include Corning, Charles Schwab, PerkinElmer Instruments, Nokia, Monsanto, Apple, GE (owing mostly to GE Capital), Roche, and Samsung. Although we have not done an exhaustive population cohort study, it would seem that only about 5 percent to 10 percent of profitable and growing companies transform or redefine their core business fundamentally in the course of a decade. Sometimes, also, the "transformations" of the day that are most well reported in the press turn out to be false—examples abound from Enron to Vivendi to AOL-Time Warner. At the same time, we also see evidence that the need and frequency to redefine the core is increasing over time due to higher levels of turbulence in most industries. Given the deep roots that a company's historic core has, it is no wonder that change of this magnitude is seldom attempted or successful.

Because redefinitions come in all shapes and sizes, we needed a working definition. We decided that a company had redefined, or transformed, its core effectively if it was experiencing profitable growth and if it had changed its business model or its business definition fundamentally. To get a sense of the range of transformations, consider the following three examples.

Marvel Entertainment: Shift to a New Business Model

Marvel Entertainment was once the leading publisher of comic books, featuring an astounding array of iconic superheroes from Spider-Man and the Incredible Hulk to Wolverine. Yet, in 1996, Marvel was in trouble, and even Spider-Man and his amazing powers could not avert the company's decline to bankruptcy. However, just as if life were imitating art, the company that created and controlled a stable of more than five thousand characters appearing in more than thirty thousand stories underwent a renewal.

The new leadership—director Isaac Perlmutter (who became CEO in 2005) and creative leader Avi Arad—saw the potential to shift this comic book publisher into a more broadly based entertainment business built around these proven and beloved superheroes. They discovered that the characters, their deep fan base, and the astonishing library of stories could be repurposed to modern times and modern media. Initially, they worked with film studios, promoting

Spider-Man, which proved to be a blockbuster success. Eventually, they worked through more and more characters—X-Men, the Fantastic Four, Silver Surfer, and so on—as well as continuing the Spider-Man movie sequels. The success of the movies spurred the sale of game products, books, and created an active online community of devoted fans. Today, Marvel has begun to produce its own movies— a new adjacency to its core—with good early success. Its first self-produced movie, *Iron Man*, pulled in $582 million at the worldwide box office, further fueling other revenue streams from toy licensing. Even the original comic book core experienced a renewal. Recently, the company announced a 2010 opening date for a Spider-Man show on Broadway called *Turn Off the Dark*.

The result has been nothing less than spectacular—a rescue befitting Marvel's superheroes. In 2008, Marvel attained revenues of $676 million and EBIT of $355 million. In the five years following December 2003, the company's stock grew by more than 58 percent while the NYSE went down 11 percent over the same period. The company has changed its business model, moved into new adjacencies, and rescued its original core in a way even Spider-Man would admire. The ultimate validation of Marvel's strategy came in August 2009, when Disney made a bid for the company and its stable of super-heroes in a deal valued at $4 billion at the time.

General Dynamics: Shrink to Grow

General Dynamics was formed in 1952 through the combination of the Electric Boat Company, a builder of submarines and ships, and Convair, a maker of aircraft. The company grew rapidly during the defense buildup of the 1960s, growing its aerospace business and developing the controversial F-111 fighter. In 1976, General Dynamics purchased the Chrysler Defense business, and in 1986, it purchased Cessna Aircraft to become a far-flung defense systems conglomerate.

In the early 1990s, General Dynamics saw the impending defense cutbacks and recognized the danger of its participation across many businesses in which it was not the leader. Although the company had grown to more than $10 billion in sales in 1990, it was about to lose money for the next three years. This crisis spurred new management to decide to re-form around its strongest core business—marine systems—and to strengthen and broaden this core.

Over the next two years, General Dynamics shrunk by 70 percent, to $3.1 billion in sales in 1995, and returned to profitability in the process. With the proceeds from the sales in missile defense and aerospace, it acquired firms that reinforced and broadened the core, such as shipbuilder Bath Iron Works. These actions propelled the revenue of General Dynamics back to $9 billion, with profits of $880 million. Investors responded well to the transformation of the company portfolio, pushing its market value from $1 billion at the start of the decade to nearly $12 billion at the end.

The casual observer of the General Dynamics story might see it as an example of a restructuring followed by renewed growth from a stronger core. And it certainly was that. However, it was much more. General Dynamics was among the first in the late 1980s to perceive the changing business model in military procurement. The fall of the Soviet Union and the dismantling of the Berlin Wall increased the pressure on defense spending. One consequence of this softening in military appropriations was the shift from cost-plus contracts, which had fueled the defense-oriented industrial establishment for decades, toward fixed-price contracts. These new contracts would put greater pressure on costs and profits. No longer would the government bear financial risk and fund growing capacity; now money would be made only by tight management of the backlog—a very different business model. The management at General Dynamics felt that many of the company's businesses had therefore reached maximum value and that potential buyers (other defense companies) were enjoying the highest cash flow they would experience for some time to come. A Bain estimate of shareholder value created by General Dynamics five years after its restructuring suggests that one-third to one-half of the $9 billion value increase came from recognizing how the new rules of the game were going to shift value and acting accordingly, with swift divestitures and restructuring. Since that time, General Dynamics has been, by many measures, among the best-performing major defense companies in the world.

Apple: Shift the Core to Drive into New Adjacencies

Perhaps the most spectacular corporate rejuvenation of the past five years is Apple. Apple redefined itself by developing a new "core" around the iPod and iTunes, driving it to leadership economics and creating a repeatable formula to expand into a range of adjacencies. However, not too long ago, Apple's original computing core was in a bad strategic situation. By the end of 2003, Apple's stock had languished for fifteen years at virtually the same level, creating no economic value. Its global market share in personal computers tumbled to 2 percent in 2004. Even during the period from 1993 through 2003, a time of intense penetration in the global use of personal computers, Apple's total return to shareholders was only 4 percent and its return on equity just 2 percent.

Yet, starting in 2003 with the launch of the iTunes Music Store, iPod sales took off. In just two years, Apple attained 70 percent of the market for portable MP3 players, and iTunes captured 85 percent of the market for music downloads. From June 2003 to May 2009, Apple's market value exploded from $7 billion to more than $100 billion. Interestingly, Apple's renewal depended on preexisting capabilities in design, technology, its young core customer base, and its superiority in developing software user interfaces. Certainly iTunes and the iPod are models of user simplicity.

Apple's adjacency expansion machine is now operating in high gear along many dimensions—new products added to iTunes such as movies and TV shows (almost unlimited in possibilities), form factors for the iPod, retail store expansion, and all the possibilities that the iPhone offers, such as the AppStore for software downloads.

These thumbnail sketches show how transformations vary along the following key dimensions:

- Method (organic versus discontinuous through acquisition)

- End result (shift versus redefine versus replace the original business model)

- Organizational structure of new core (integrated versus separate)

- Role of technology (limited versus decisive)

- Rationale (turnaround versus defensive versus offensive)

In a recent analysis of more than forty transformations, a Bain & Company team found that, beyond the obvious ingredients such as the "right strategy" or capability or resources, several controllable variables drove success. These variables had strong statistical correlation with outcome and ultimate economic returns. In order of average importance, they were:

1. Short time frame and sense of immediacy

2. Clear motivating rationale for the "point of arrival"

3. Strong, committed, and visible CEO leadership

4. Strong economic stake in the result for management

5. Willingness to change or replace management as necessary

Some of these findings, such as emphasis on a short time frame and willingness to destabilize the team, contradict perceived wisdom—yet they are echoed in the practices of the best private equity firms.

The Actuarial Tables of Corporate Mortality

Most biological species, including humans, achieve longer life spans with each successive generation. The opposite appears to be true for companies: Corporate mortality and morbidity tables would show that companies' life spans are shortening and their health is more frequently imperiled, due largely to failure to adapt to rapidly changing environments.

In his work on the "living company," Arie de Geus assembled corporate population statistics suggesting that the average life expectancy of corporations in the Northern Hemisphere is well under twenty years. Only the large corporations he studied, which had started to expand after they survived high-risk infancy, continued to live on average another twenty to thirty years.[3] These findings are consistent with those of other studies of corporate life expectancy. For instance, the *Economist* cites statistics suggesting that the average European and Japanese company now survives less than thirteen years.[4]

De Geus also studied closely twenty-seven companies that survived more than one hundred years, led by Stora, the Swedish paper and chemical company that is more than seven hundred years old. In all cases, he found that longevity hinged on the companies' ability to transform their core business at a few critical times. In fact, de Geus found that all twenty-seven companies turned over their complete business portfolio, on average, at least once in their lifetime. Their ability to shift and migrate their core business, to adapt to their environment, ultimately determined their survival.[5] As Charles Darwin said of species, "It is not the strongest species that survive, nor the most intelligent, but the ones most adaptive to change." The same appears true of companies.

The Increasing Odds of Corporate Morbidity

Every insurance actuary keeps not only mortality tables showing average life spans, but also morbidity tables showing rates of crippling injury and ill health. Much of our analysis revealed the large proportion of companies whose rate of return went through long periods at less than their cost of capital. Many of them, such as

National Semiconductor, Westinghouse, Sears, U.S. Steel, Xerox, or General Motors, are companies that once possessed the lion's share of value in their industry. Now they are seeing that pool of profits shift to new competitors and more adaptive historic rivals.

One predictor of corporate morbidity might be the rate at which the profit pool in any given industry is shifting. Whereas even a couple of decades ago company value moved like molasses, today it flows like quicksilver—as recent experiences in financial services, newspapers, and telecommunications, for instance, have shown. Even apart from the volatile shifts in value, there is evidence that economic value vested in a leading company has grown more tenuous. Take, for example, the jockeying for position among the top three companies during the last two decades in a sample of industries. Seventy-five percent of the industries we studied had increased rates of churn, which threatened or displaced the leader. The conclusion: Leaders can lose position more easily than ever, and they do.

We also looked at the distribution of economic value across companies in these industries from the mid-1980s to 2000. Here, more than 70 percent of the total industry value (measured by share of total value) had changed hands or shifted across a wide range of industries, including health care providers, steel, computers, mobile phones, and mass retailing.

Most large companies are finding it increasingly difficult to maintain value. During the twenty-five years between 1958 and 1983, fully 70 percent of the twenty most valuable companies in the United States remained on the list. By contrast, over the next twenty-five years, from 1983 to 2008, only 30 percent managed to stay on the list.

The Chances of Succeeding at Redefinition

The statistics on company life span and the rate at which leaders lose their place in times of turbulence provide stark evidence that redefining a strong core business is tricky. To gain greater insight into the odds of success and failure in business redefinition, we selected twenty companies that were leaders or strong performers in their core business and were profitable at the start of a period of turbulence in their particular industries. All twenty failed to seize the initiative to adapt and, as a result, performed worse after the turbulent period than before. Either new competitors emerged or strong followers took advantage of the leaders' inability to change fast enough.

This analysis included companies such as Digital Equipment Corporation and IBM (encountering the PC revolution), Tandy (encountering the information systems changes facilitating big-box retailers), McDonnell Douglas (encountering the rationalization of its core Defense Department customers), Xerox (encountering the radical shifts to digital information and networking), Kodak (encountering the entrance of a foreign competitor combined with the advent of digital imaging), and Delta Air Lines and United Airlines (encountering airline deregulation). Virtually none of our leaders improved their performance after the turbulence, despite an upswing in the macroeconomy worldwide. Rather, the financial returns to shareholders of these companies eroded by an average of more than ten points per year and moved from above to below the cost of capital. We found that companies often expanded aggressively into adjacencies when the more overwhelming imperative for them would have been to continue to focus on exploiting, reinforcing, and strengthening their core. Our previously cited examples of Bausch & Lomb, Sears, and WH Smith illustrate this danger.

The most devastating mismatch of strategy and growth cycle is found in the company that needs to redefine some fundamental aspects of its core business but instead, aware or unaware of the threat, continues to attempt expansion with its old model. Consider the following examples:

- Sears watched The Home Depot, with its low-cost and superior-service business model, sell hardware (the core of the Sears retail store) as it grew from one to ten to fifty to two hundred stores. Only when The Home Depot had become a $10 billion company did Sears began aggressively experimenting with alternative retail formats. But by then it was too late to stem the competition, which today is led by Lowe's.

• Kodak had somewhat accurate forecasts of the rate at which digital camera usage would penetrate into film technologies across its major business areas, yet was not able to define its plan, mobilize its organization, and wean itself off the lucrative cash flow from film rapidly enough. By early 2009, despite herculean efforts, the company that once dominated its industry is worth only $700 million, significantly less than what it was worth at its peak, despite the fact that the total world photography industry profit pool is several times larger.

Redefinition Is About Speed

If speed were not an issue, core businesses could be continually repositioned through adjacency expansion as described in the previous chapter. However, when turbulence hits, typical organizational and strategic responses may not be fast enough for three reasons:

1. Major change programs that take too long to complete have a poor track record of results.

2. The capital markets penalize slow response to turbulence.

3. Slow response to turbulence can erode competitive position.

Lengthy change programs do not command organizational focus and attention. To understand this better, we examined twenty major transformation programs—both turnaround and new-growth strategies. The programs that were substantially completed in fewer than fifteen months yielded returns three times higher than the programs that took three years.

During the 1980s, reengineering caught corporate attention as a panacea to reverse slowing growth and fill emerging gaps in profit. Entire consulting firms rose and fell on the back of these major reengineering programs intended to transform corporations, eliminate layers, speed decision-making processes, and take advantage of new information technologies.

Reengineering attempted to make major change in core business processes done from the inside, rewiring the engine while it was functioning. Today the record shows that more than 70 percent of these programs were worthless or destroyed value, and that many of the rest fell far short of their targets.[6] Indeed, even one of the early architects of the reengineering wave, Michael Hammer, did research at the Center for Corporate Change that documents failure rates of this sort. John Kotter, at the Harvard Business School, also studied more than 280 change programs and found a failure rate of more than 90 percent. The primary reasons for failure are a lack of urgency and of sustained energy and commitment to the required level of change once the difficulty and cost become apparent. This, of course, relates to time involved. In any organization, it is simply impossible to maintain a state of crisis and intensity over a period of two to three years. Yet the inherent complexity of reengineering made it difficult to implement large-scale programs in less time. The failure rate of reengineering was almost preordained by the basics of human behavior.

The rest of this chapter explores this phenomenon of redefinition and addresses three key questions:

1. How do I know when it may be time to redefine my core business?

2. What are the best organizational methods for tackling this difficult task?

3. What are the lessons learned from past successes and failures at redefining a core business?

When to Redefine the Core

Imagine senior executives' response to the following developments:

- A large long-distance carrier, constantly claiming to its share-holders that Internet telephony was far in the future, discovers that quality is improving faster than expected and the usage of "free" long-distance phone calls is increasing faster than anticipated. What will create the profit streams of the future, you wonder?

- A large insurance company that knows all of its profits come from price variations and market imperfections in consumer knowledge sees a growing share of its customers pricing insurance on the Internet, exposing the company's price inefficiency to public view, and perhaps exposing its lack of real marketplace differentiation. What can you do to create a more viable source of future profitability?

- A newspaper hovering near breakeven analyzes its declining classified advertising revenues and readership only to find that the shift to online sources by younger readers has accelerated and that advertising is moving away from the print newspaper faster than had been forecast. These changes are draining the paper's coffers of revenue, and there are fewer funds to invest in the future. What do you do now?

- A regional retail chain selling pet products discovers that Wal-Mart stores are moving into its market and that Wal-Mart is investing to expand its pet section. Early evidence indicates that Wal-Mart is gaining market share, but competing just on price is to play their game. How can you change the core to be differentiated in the future against Wal-Mart's form of retail mechanized warfare?

- A major bricks-and-mortar book retailer realizes that the 20 percent to 30 percent discount offered online is not a temporary phenomenon and that new consumer devices like the Kindle, which allow readers to download books, are improving and gaining consumer acceptance. What do you do?

These and thousands of other scenarios are illustrations of once-strong, focused core businesses recognizing the probable need to redefine their core in a fundamental way and grappling with how and when to do so.

Consider core redefinition in the case of Xerox. Xerox traces the roots of its core business back to electrophotography patents filed by Chester Carlson in the late 1930s. Trying to get his ideas funded, Carlson approached a long list of companies, including RCA, Remington Rand, General Electric, Kodak, and IBM. They all turned him down, content to stick with carbon paper. Subsequent decades would see the creation of Xerox and the gradual development of xerography up to the launch of the revolutionary 914 copier in 1959. This product transformed the copying industry, driving out of business more than thirty companies that primarily used mimeography, carbon paper, and diazo printing. The 914 truly detonated major industry turbulence—and growth. In the 1950s, offices in the United States made approximately 20 million copies, in tedious and slow ways. With Xerox machines, the number of copies exploded to 14 billion in 1966 and more than 700 billion by 1985.

For a time, Xerox held a virtual monopoly. But attacks from the bottom of the market by Japanese manufacturer Canon, followed by Minolta, Ricoh, and Sharp, triggered a decade of attack and counterattack by Xerox. From 1976 to 1982, Xerox saw its worldwide share of copier revenues decline from 82 percent to 40 percent.[7] Xerox's return to shareholders dropped to near breakeven. The company fought in the traditional manner of an awakened leader combating relatively traditional forms of competition in a well-defined business.

Today, Xerox machines compete for share of document reproduction with more powerful faxes, high-speed printers connected to computers, scanners connected to printers, and e-mail. A clearly defined business has become much more complex and the boundaries increasingly fuzzy. The convergence of technologies means that Xerox's key competitor may now be Hewlett-Packard in the broad arena of digital document management, a much expanded business definition.

Warning Signs of Industry Transformation

More passengers are killed or injured from turbulence in the air than from any other aviation hazard. With the exception of sudden wind shear, most turbulence can be seen and predicted with sophisticated Doppler radar detectors. Even wind shear instrumentation is developing rapidly. What are the warning signs for business of pending turbulence and the need to change course?

There are several telltale signs of looming turbulence that should be tracked by the radar of companies that want to maintain profitable growth of a core business. In fact, our examination of twenty-five instances of turbulence (excluding Internet-related ones) that have played out until the period of the financial crisis of 2008 indicates that the storm clouds on the horizon throw distinct, observable shadows at our feet. Advance warning of turbulence in each case was one of the following conditions.

Erosion of Low-end Product Segments. This turbulence starts, seemingly innocuously, with the washing away of market share of a low-end customer segment that was deemed unprofitable and difficult to serve. This is the "innovator's dilemma" written about by Clayton Christensen, where a new, disruptive technology with new, low-cost economics appears on the scene that makes the least profitable and desirable customers of the leader suddenly profitable and interesting to the new follower. By successively ceding low-end market segments, incumbents can back themselves into a corner. An example is the penetration of electronic trading in securities, a channel initially scorned by leading brokerage houses such as Bear Stearns and Merrill Lynch.

In the steel industry, these dynamics played out twice in rapid succession. In the 1980s came the entrance of low-cost Japanese steel manufactured by continuous casting. The Japanese, too, worked their way up the value chain in steel, starting with low-end commodity slabs and coils and moving to higher-margin product. Five years later, new competitors entered the industry, such as Nucor Corporation and Worthington Steel, both of which achieved lower costs in very small-scale production through minimill technology.

Core Customer Defection. This form of turbulence first becomes apparent in increased customer defections. For example, consumers in the automobile industry indicate a 70 percent to 80 percent satisfaction rate with their cars. Yet more than half of car buyers switch brands at their next purchase. Satisfaction measures simply reflect customers' rationalizations of their past decisions. Defection or loyalty measures reflect consumers' actual behavior and reveal their true satisfaction. Loyalty data on consumers' reactions to small Japanese cars in the 1980s stands in stark contrast to the data from satisfaction surveys that anaesthetized leaders during this period, such as General Motors, to their untenable status quo strategy. Sudden changes in core defection rates of once loyal customers spell trouble.

Erosion of Microsegments. One of the most corrosive dangers for a company is the emergence of a new competitor that can attack underserved microsegments of a customer base with a targeted and superior model. This danger is hard to detect and can signal a fundamental shift in the nature of competition. The Internet is sometimes credited primarily with revolutionizing commoditization and direct selling. In fact, the opposite is true. The Internet has laid slick tracks for microsegmentation and the emergence of true and more subtle product differentiation and customization. This means Internet innovations often glide to market with a stealth that ambushes traditional competitors.

In the 1970s, ABC, CBS, and NBC accounted for 94 percent of the television viewing audience in the United States. Today, the combined network share of viewers is much less. The difference is made up by hundreds of "narrowcasters," such as a golf station, CNN, ethnic stations, religious stations, science stations, sports stations, shopping stations, kids' stations, and so on. The great audience erosion from CBS News to CNN constitutes a microcosm of too-long-ignored opportunities unearthed by microsegmentation.

Erosion of Traditional Business Boundaries. Perhaps the most obvious, but also the most often denied, sign of change is the sudden erosion of traditional business boundaries, in effect doubling (or more) the number of competitors vying for a space. The advent of digital imagery, for instance, is a transformational threat to Xerox in the market for reproduction and to traditional film and camera manufacturers in the market for photography.

New Intermediaries and New Control Points. Some of the most profitable businesses over time have been those that were able to control a position in a larger system that others needed to pass through, pass over, or use in some manner. Physical control points ranging from the Port of Venice, which controlled the ocean-borne spice trade to Europe in the 1400s, to the Panama Canal are physical examples. Electronic examples range from Microsoft's stranglehold over the personal computer industry by virtue of its proprietary DOS operating system to Ticketmaster's dominance in selling tickets to certain events online.

Internet-Induced Turbulence

The Internet is driving quick and dramatic change because it facilitates lower transactions costs, distributes ubiquitous information, and enables the creation of networks. Even though it's been a decade since the burst of the dot-com bubble, the Internet continues to drive new forms of real and profound structural change in businesses with high information costs relative to total costs throughout the value chain, and with high potential for reducing transactions costs or obliterating unneeded steps. The impact of the Internet on company structure can be especially profound where there are many buyers and sellers, bringing communications and network effects into play. A portfolio of businesses can be identified and categorized according to its areas for greatest Internet-induced change.

In one situation, the primary impact of change comes from new productivity sources. An example might be Cisco, the leading supplier of Internet equipment. Recognizing the business power of the Internet, Cisco quickly moved to transact 85 percent of its revenue over the Web. More important, the wide range of Internet-enabled productivity improvements has allowed the company to become a cost leader. In software, Oracle is the leader in Web enablement and has reduced its costs by $1 billion.

Most companies can profit from a second situation, where the Internet enables new growth from the core assets. U.S. West's yellow page advertising business benefited from such improvements. The company transformed its large field sales force from one solely focused on printed advertisements to one that also sells ads on the Internet and provides a substantial array of services and home-page assistance to small businesses. Already, this initiative has boosted the bottom line.

In the third situation, opportunities occur in business models where information costs are especially high. Examples include the distribution of books or electronic parts, in which search costs are large relative to the prices of the item and the customer and supplier bases are diffuse.

Litmus Tests for Redefinition

How do you know when it is time to decide whether a major redefinition of the core is in order? Our research shows that management teams often see the change coming and forecast its course quite precisely, but ultimately have difficulty deciding how to change and how to mobilize the organization. For instance, Kodak had relatively clear forecasts of the future course of digital technology in its major businesses. But, given the complexity and magnitude of the required change, the company had difficulty mobilizing fast—and it struggled to wean itself off a robust cash stream from film. It failed to determine early the shape of the new Kodak. Meanwhile, more nimble competitors and new competitors moved ahead at a faster rate. The same is true in newspapers, music, or telecoms. The difficulty of these dilemmas of redefinition is also seen in the auto industry over a period of decades, culminating only now in a rash of bankruptcies and near bankruptcies of major car companies in America. Yet, the seeds of this failure were sown decades ago—and still the industry changed too little and too slowly by most standards. No single formula can be applied to these complex situations, but we have used the following litmus tests for determining when serious consideration of redefinition may be in order:

- Are top-tier venture capitalists funding businesses with the avowed intent of attacking a segment of your core business? If yes, drill down further.

- Are sophisticated recruits in interview discussions elsewhere in the industry asking tougher and tougher questions about your fundamental business model? If yes, assume they know something from their discussions.

- Is a new competitor beginning to gain surprisingly rapid market share in a marginal segment of your business that you once controlled? If yes, remember that many of the most disruptive technologies began to develop and spread in this way.

- Are steps in the value chain that you once considered core now being unbundled and controlled by specialists? If yes, then market power may shift to a player that captures and locks up a critical step, achieving a gatekeeper status to the rest of the industry.

Are there fast-growing adjacent customer segments that you might once have been able to serve but that you could not now compete for without adding a new capability? If yes, then immediately study these customers and understand what is going on.

Are there potential legal or regulatory changes that could eviscerate your competitive position in the core or your ability to compete for the next set of logical business adjacencies in your growth plan? If yes, then immediately formulate contingency plans to hedge against this uncertainty.

If the answer to two or more of the above questions is yes, the odds are that you should seriously consider realigning your core.

Preparing the Organization to Redefine the Core

Redefining a core business while still running it profitably poses several immediate and nontrivial dilemmas that are especially acute with many Internet-driven redefinitions:

- *Pricing.* To make the new model fully competitive requires developing different pricing strategies. But what does that do to the core business?

- *Staffing.* The new model of the core requires excellent managers to execute a difficult start-up and ensure that the company competes effectively. But the best managers are needed to run the original core, where all the profits come from historically.

- *Rewards.* The reward structure may need to be different in the newly redefined model. But how can all employees be motivated equitably?

- *Channels.* Selling a product in a way that competes with historic channel relationships is disorienting and difficult for the original core. But that core frequently holds the power.

- *Success.* Suppose that the new model is successful and begins to gain market share. What tensions does this cause during the transition phase, and can they be managed internally?

More than ever before, companies are grappling with the tension between redefining the core internally, to retain the value of one integrated business and set of customers, and redefining it externally, to allow independent strategies and attract the right kind of talent. Before launching into redefinition (assuming a concept of the new model and strategy), you must confront this choice and carefully work through its implications.

Waking Up to Core Redefinition

One day you wake up to discover that your core business will be at a severe disadvantage in the future because of changes in technology or customer needs or new competitive forces. Moreover, you find that these changes are occurring so rapidly that merely repositioning the core through either a series of adjacency moves or a limited acquisition is too slow a proposition. What is the best way, you ask yourself, to begin to reshape, or redefine, the core quickly while still making money in the original business in its original form?

First, identify which of three basic situations your company is in, as depicted in figure 4-2. The first is where a core business, serving a core set of known customers, is confronted with a radically improved business model for serving its current core customers' needs. Examples of such "frontal assaults" on companies' cores abound. The emergence of Staples, with a cost model for delivering office products 15 percent lower than that of traditional stationers, was one. The rise of Dell Computer, with its direct model superiority over traditional suppliers in the 1990s was another. Hewlett-Packard's use of low-cost, distributed printing of digitized documents, bypassing xerography, was a third. Still another was the emergence of Charles Schwab using online trading to displace competitors by doing trades at a fraction of the cost of a traditional transaction. Google's assault on the search business with a superior technology is another. The emergence

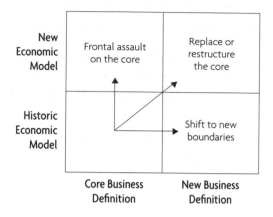

New
Economic
Model

| Frontal assault on the core | Replace or restructure the core |

Historic
Economic
Model

| | Shift to new boundaries |

Core Business
Definition

New Business
Definition

4-2 Companies Must Redefine Their Cores

of low-cost airlines is a case of such a frontal assault: They create havoc for bookings and pricing of traditional carriers.

The second situation is where the original boundaries and structure of the core business are changing in complicated ways. An example of shifting boundaries is in the newspaper business. Once the local newspaper (like the *Rocky Mountain News*, Denver's oldest newspaper, with roots back to 1859, which was shuttered in 2009) competed almost entirely against its cross-town rival. Today, the game has changed. Information is unbundled on the Internet and delivered instantly at low cost to almost any location. A recent survey conducted of the youngest people at Bain & Company showed that in most geographies, virtually no one went first to the newspaper for many categories of information (current headlines, sports scores, movie listings, weather, stock quotes, classifieds, and so on) that used to be the bread and butter of the newspaper. Competitors now range from local community websites to Yahoo.com to ESPN and CNN.com, and, increasingly, Google. The Kindle user can now download an increasingly large number of global newspapers, turning the local newspaper competition even more global. Once traditional and quite simple boundaries are now fuzzy and covered by a proliferation of new competitors. These complex and confusing situations are especially difficult to mobilize against, since the new competitors are less well known and the path forward is often unclear and confused by a wide range of nonobvious choices.

The third situation is where turbulence could remove the need for the core, thereby emasculating it over time. For instance, video rental stores, in the long term, face such a threat from on-demand electronic delivery of movies. In the last two years, major chains have been shrinking, and one entered and emerged from bankruptcy. The leader, Blockbuster, has an increasingly fragile financial base.

The methods for fundamentally redefining a core business range broadly and are expanding all the time as the business community experiments with new ways to accomplish what was once a seldom-required initiative. Common methods include restructuring through divestiture, acquisition, or reverse merger as well as the more organic methods arrayed in figure 4-3, which spans the spectrum from changing the core processes from within to spinning off a new core into a separate company with professional outside investors. Figure 4-4 summarizes the trade-offs between integration and separation.

We have been involved with numerous clients wrestling with these trade-offs and have seen situations where each has been judged to be on the right or the wrong path to redefinition, given their specific time pressures and competitive threats.

Situation 1: Frontal Assault on the Core Business Model

The primary considerations in mobilizing to a direct assault on your core by a "new to world" business model are reaction speed, how you choose to deal with cannibalization of the original (perhaps very profitable) core, and the linkage between the original core business and the model for the future. There is no single best answer for all cases. For instance, one study that focused on the telecom, photonics, and computer-hardware industries found that willingness to set up structures that cannibalize the core business in

4-3 Methods for Redefining the Core Lie along a Spectrum

Integrate ← → Separate

| Integrate the idea into the core | Create a separate unit within the same division | Create a separate unit with parallel reporting to CEO | Create a corporate incubator | Spin off the idea as a wholly owned business | Spin off the idea with a corporate partner | Spin off the idea with a venture capital partner | Establish a joint venture with outside incubation | Sell the idea |

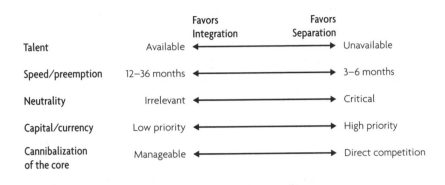

	Favors Integration		Favors Separation	
Talent	Available	←	→	Unavailable
Speed/preemption	12–36 months	←	→	3–6 months
Neutrality	Irrelevant	←	→	Critical
Capital/currency	Low priority	←	→	High priority
Cannibalization of the core	Manageable	←	→	Direct competition

4-4 Redefining the Core Involves Making Trade-offs

an orderly manner was the differentiator between companies that successfully navigated through turbulence and those that didn't.[8] Redefinitions that change a highly strategic, core process and require integration into the core business are often best done internally. One example is Kodak's initiatives to shift to digital processing capabilities in its labs, with a range of new Internet services for processing digital images. Another example is ING Direct, the first and most successful implementation of an online banking business. The venture was originally set up as quite separate from the ING banking core, with even a separate advisory board, treasury, and launch plan to manage cannibalization. However, as ING Direct gained momentum, it increasingly integrated with the core bank, and in some geographies is now shaping the nature of new, more automated branches—a hybrid of pure online and traditional retail.

When the new business is strongly related to the core, but will never replace the original business, the best decision will rest on tactical trade-offs inherent in answers to the following:

- Is the new business better able to attract the talent it needs as an integrated entity or as an autonomous unit?

- Would the new business model receive a high valuation from the external stock market, and is such currency required to buy talent and invest in the business?

- Would separating the new business from the old foster the competition necessary to define customer boundaries where one model is superior to the other?

Based on its answers to these questions, Staples.com, the online version of the office superstore Staples, chose to design and launch itself initially as a separate Internet business. Staples, one of the great business success stories of the past two decades, is now the market leader in the sale of office supplies and was one of the fastest companies to grow to $10 billion. In order to stake out this territory ahead of a variety of nascent online competitors, Staples set up Staples.com as a separate company in a physical location adjacent to the corporate headquarters. The start-up had about one hundred employees, whose mission was to sell an expanded version of the Staples product line over the Internet, with deliveries arranged from Staples's core distribution system. Staples.com was to be issued to the public as a tracking stock whose value was established in an initial round of funding by a 5 percent sale of the business to several venture capitalists. Founder Tom Stemberg and the Staples management team believed that this approach would attract talent and develop a separate Internet culture, thereby getting the company off to a quick start.

The Staples management team took several additional steps to balance the core with the need for independence. First, it established transfer prices for corporate services and products consistent with the costs to the retail stores and the wholesale channels. Second, it distributed stock options not only to the employees of the start-up, but to the employees in the parent company, all the way through to the retail store staff. Finally, it encouraged competition for the total customer base, discovering that the best accounts are those that buy through all channels and modes.

Situation 2: Shifting Resources to a New Business Definition

Sometimes redefining the core entails making a change in the boundaries that define the business, requiring the establishment of a new entity that draws on skills and assets from the core but does not anticipate cannibalizing it extensively. There are three types of boundary changes: (1) the development of new intermediaries, such as online auctions and exchanges, enabled by information technology; (2) the unbundling of the traditional value chain into its constituent activities (the outsourcing wave of the past decade and the rise of major Indian companies like Infosys testifies to the power of this form of redefinition); and (3) the radical and rapid broadening of customer product and service offerings enabled by a new technology (an example is the sequence of product launch announcements by Apple surrounding iTunes and new content, iPod and new form factors, and iPhone with its new applications).

New businesses that draw heavily on the core, but will not cannibalize the core to a great degree, are often best set up in separate units. Whether these units should be outside of the corporate structure and with outside ownership is primarily a function of three trade-offs:

1. Can the right talent be attracted inside, and is the existence or prospect of an initial public offering required to attract this talent?

2. Is separation required for strategic reasons, which generally stem from the need for neutrality or the need to avoid creating conflict with customers in the core business (such as competing with customers or with the channel)?

3. Would separation provide a source of public financing, because of high stock valuations, for making critical strategic acquisitions or investments?

Situation 3: Structural Redefinition of the Core

Economist Joseph Schumpeter, writing during the 1940s, argued that the earnings ability of any industrial concern diminishes over time. We would extend this observation to say that today, any core business that does not change fundamentally from time to time is bound to see its earnings capacity and its competitive position decline.

Sometimes redefining the core requires a rapid and massive redeployment of resources from the historic business to a promising adjacency. Earlier in the book, we noted that only about 3 percent of our sustained value creating companies were "shrinking value creators." Several of these companies made major structural changes to sell and replace their original core business, effectively reforming the company around a new core. PerkinElmer Instruments provides an example of a dramatic companywide redefinition of a core business from basic laboratory analytical instruments to instruments that analyze the sequencing of genes for biotechnology.

When Tony White took over Perkin-Elmer Corporation in 1995, the company was valued at $1.5 billion, and it consisted primarily of a wide range of niche-focused analytical instruments accumulated in the portfolio since its founding in 1932 by Richard Perkin and Charles Elmer. The original business, built on optical instrumentation, eventually extended from bombsights to satellite reconnaissance devices. The loose collection of businesses prompted some investors to suggest the company liquidate its product lines one by one to the highest bidder.

In the array of Perkin-Elmer's businesses, White noticed a small business that sold instruments that could perform high-speed genetic mapping and sequencing and was the apparent leader in its small but promising niche. Over the next few years, the Perkin-Elmer team streamlined the original core businesses for sale to EG&G, a provider of management and technical services to governmental agencies, and shifted its investment resources to the gene-sequencing business, catching a research wave that carried biosystems revenues from $320 million to $1.2 billion in three years. White then split the company into PE Biosystems, the equipment manufacturer, and Celera Genomics, a sequencing business that buys and runs the sequencing equipment.

By 2006, PE Biosystems (then called Applied Biosystems, or ABS) and Celera were worth more than $6 billion in total market capitalization, multiples of the value of the original Perkin-Elmer that White inherited. But that was not the end of the transformation. In November 2008, Applied Biosystems merged with Invitrogen in a deal valued at $6.7 billion. The result is Life Technologies, the largest "pure play" company by an order of magnitude in the field of genomics and genetic detection with market leadership both in the sequencing analysis equipment and in the consumable supplies needed for genetic analysis.

The seminal insight of the ABS management team was in seeing the full potential of the genetic-mapping business and in brilliantly redeploying and executing a complex strategy to shift the whole company's center of gravity. Beginning with a gem buried deep in the portfolio, they took advantage of a rapidly transforming market for biotechnology equipment and a powerful hidden asset in their core business.

Sometimes redefinition by structural change takes longer, involving a much more extensive sequence of exits and capability acquisitions. Such a strategy comes with a high level of difficulty—and high failure rate. Still, there are some striking examples of success, few more so than Nokia.

Nokia began in 1865 as a mill for the manufacture of pulp and paper on the Nokia River in Finland. During the next 130 years, the company accumulated a range of regional industrial companies, creating a small conglomerate with businesses ranging from paper to electronics to rubber. In fact, rubber boots in Finland are still referred to as *nokia*. Nokia's transformation came from an inseparable combination of opportunism, smart decisions, and good fortune. In 1982, the company's leadership decided to work with the Finnish telecommunications industry to implement the first countrywide mobile phone system using the GSM standard. The first wireless phone call ever made was placed on this GSM system by the Finnish prime minister in 1991.

From then on, Nokia's leadership, especially its new CEO Jorma Ollila, saw the confluence of wireless technology and digital information as the place to begin betting the company. For the next few years, Ollila invested aggressively in plants to produce handsets and acquisitions to support the emerging telecommunications strategy. Nokia financed these investments by divesting many of its other businesses in rubber, cable, color TV, and energy. The cell phone story is still playing out technologically and competitively, but it fueled Nokia's growth from just $2 billion of revenues in 1993 to $66 billion in 2008, with margins that increased steadily. From almost nowhere, Nokia has captured 37 percent of the world cellular phone handset market, making it the clear leader. Granted, the company enjoyed good fortune in several respects: For instance, it invested in a cellular start-up at the right time, and GSM was a robust European standard in contrast to the balkanized North American systems. Nonetheless, Nokia remains a remarkable story of using acquisition to transform, indeed replace, an original core.

Other companies, such as Monsanto and Cisco, also have relied on buying and selling to create a strong core. But more, including Xerox, Sears, General Motors, Westinghouse, Zenith, and Olivetti, have fallen short. The approach takes time—and who is to say you will guess right? In all of these cases, the transformation of the core resulted in new companies with a highly focused, new core business targeting leadership in a market with new definition and boundaries. Structural redefinitions of the core are not options that always, or even frequently, make sense. They require the confluence of several preconditions: the ideal core to migrate toward, a market growth environment where investors reward preemptive moves, a management team with a clear vision of a new future, and above all, the team's ability to execute highly difficult strategy.

Conclusion

Industry turbulence is hitting more rapidly and powerfully than ever. Our data shows that decision times are shortening, uncertainty is increasing, and the range of fundamental strategic choices is widening. Many of the changes faced by executives require partial or complete rethinking of the fundamentals of their core business.

In some cases, the required actions call for rapidly redefining part of the core, as the leaders of Marvel Entertainment did, or shifting resources to an entirely new core, as the leaders of PerkinElmer did. We have attempted to identify a wide range of successful cases of companies redefining their core business. Yet, we found many more instances of companies falling short. Redefinition is hard: Most managers have never done it before, and it entails high risk. The success cases cited suggest a few instructive caveats:

1. Do not redefine the core without a clear vision and set of strategic principles on which the management team agrees.

2. Do not redefine the core without first establishing a common point of view on how turbulence might play out and what positioning in the marketplace provides the greatest competitive advantage.

3. Explore the full range of structural options to balance the need for integration with the original core and the need for speed, which can be achieved with a separate entity.

4. Overinvest in management capacity and management processes at the start of a redefinition program.

5. Recognize the inherent uncertainty that has triggered the need to consider redefining a core business, which may require hedging strategies and diagnostics for constantly measuring the "strategic dashboard" and making midcourse corrections.

Most managers have quarterly earnings to deliver, core business cash flows to protect, employees in the original core who demand fair treatment, management team members with different points of view on the future, doubts of their own about the success of redefinition, and concerns about the complexity of execution. The low success rate of redefinition to date is rarely, in our experience, due to unskilled management; it is inherent in the complexity of the task. Even to attempt to redefine business fundamentals in a world where all systems act to protect and cling to the status quo calls for extraordinary leadership. It is here that we see most acutely our third paradox of growth: It is the management teams for which the cost of inaction is the greatest that often have the most difficulty embarking on a path to redefine their core. The true heroes of the corporate world are those who successfully take on the challenges of long-term change in the face of enormous short-term pressures to cling to the status quo for yet one more quarter.

5

Growing from the Core

The research underlying this book on how companies grow shows clearly just how difficult it is to build, to maintain, and especially to transform a strong core business over a period of more than a few years. Some of the contributors to the thinking in this book are among the most talented and hardworking people we know. They have gathered around them extraordinary teams. Yet all have encountered downturns in the growth cycles of businesses in which they have been involved. So too, the greatest pilots have encountered turbulence, and the greatest coaches have had losing seasons. It is with this perspective that we regard our effort in this book. We do not suggest a formula for success—for there is none—but rather provide some strategic principles and self-diagnostic tools as references for even the most excellent managers of the strongest core businesses who must reconsider or reformulate their strategies. We believe that the principles described in this book can improve the odds of success but that no single set of ideas can guarantee it.

The research for this book has been conducted over a period of time that spans the height of private equity investing, the dawn of and early returns from the Internet economy, and one of the deepest recessions the world has ever experienced. Under all of these conditions, we have asked ourselves repeatedly whether the new ordering of leaders and followers might embody lessons that fundamentally change our thesis. The conclusion: Although we repeatedly witness a fundamental change in the way capital flows, valuations are made, and business is conducted, our central themes remain rock solid:

- Very few companies actually grow profitably and sustainably, though all plan to do so.

- Building unique strength in a core business, no matter how small or narrowly focused, is the key to subsequent growth. Many companies that neglect this principal retrench and return to the core. In fact, sometimes the right strategy is even to "shrink to grow," going back to the core of the core.

- Most management teams underestimate the growth potential of their core and fail to mine all of its hidden value growth. In fact, the best core businesses are often the greatest underperformers relative to their true potential—a phenomenon that we have called the *paradox of leadership*.

- Most successful companies achieve most of their growth by expanding into logical adjacencies that have shared economics and reinforce the core business, not from unrelated diversifications or moves into "hot" markets.

- The best route to sustained and profitable growth is expansion into a series of adjacencies using a repeatable formula, built from the most differentiating elements of a strong core.

- Many of the most damaging mistakes in strategy derive from lack of self-awareness in the core, not from external events or competitive moves.

- Industry turbulence often demands that the leader redefine his or her company's core business at a time when it appears at the height of its power. This "crisis of the core" is one of the most difficult problems in business; few companies have navigated through it well.

- As simple as it sounds, achieving growth is hard because most organizations protect the status quo, and growth requires change.

These principles come as no surprise, but it is shocking to realize how often they are violated and how often they constitute the fulcrum of the most important issues of growth strategy.

Although these principles have not changed, their specific action implications in some sectors of the economy have. Throughout our book, we have described contemporary adaptations of these principles, some of which are only now emerging or being debated. An example is the discussion about when to separate or integrate a new, possibly competitive business model.

Trigger Point for Shifting Emphasis

When is it appropriate to shift financial and management resources from the core business to surrounding adjacencies? Even more difficult, what are the warning signs that signal the need to shift a fundamental element in the core business? The constant tension between mining the core and breaking out into something new exists in every business. The way the management team deals with this tension is a key determinant of the prospects for future sustained, profitable growth.

Figure 5-1 is based on our data on more than five thousand companies used throughout this book to study the incidence of profitable growth worldwide. The figure shows the total ten-year return to shareholders from various combinations of growth in earnings and growth in revenue. Companies that grow neither earnings nor revenue at more than 10 percent earn modest returns, averaging 7 percent. Companies that achieve growth of more than 10 percent in earnings and revenue benefit from a multiplier effect, earning ten-year shareholder returns of 17.7 percent.

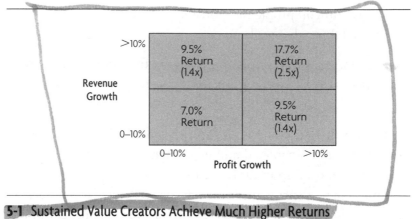

5-1 Sustained Value Creators Achieve Much Higher Returns

Source: Worldscope database; Bain analysis, 2009

Note: All growth rates are real. Number of companies = 853. Annual total shareholder return is calculated as compound annual total shareholder return over the ten-year period 1997–2007.

But particularly interesting, from the point of view of our discussion of tension between core focus and adjacency growth, are the companies represented by the two other cells in the figure. Companies with earnings of more than 10 percent, but revenues below that rate, usually expand their margin by mining the core for cost reductions. These companies receive relatively low rewards from the stock market, only 2.5 percentage points above the companies that grow neither earnings nor revenues above 10 percent. Indeed, a ten-year record of 10 percent or more earnings growth in a company with low revenue growth will yield a shareholder return of only 9.5 percent on average. This is the challenge many large core businesses face in setting budgets and earnings targets; it is usually easier year after year to mine the core for twelve more months. Yet, at some point, margin expansion potential ends. Then what?

Finally, consider companies that expand into adjacencies aggressively—possibly too aggressively—diluting the quality of their earnings and creating larger but less profitable companies. These companies grew revenues over ten years by more than 10 percent but achieved earnings growth of less than 10 percent, seeing their margins steadily decline due to their movement into new business areas in which they had less expertise and that offered less profitability. Literally thousands of companies follow this pattern. The stories of some, such as Anheuser-Busch, Mattell, Citibank, Vivendi, Bausch & Lomb, and Saatchi & Saatchi, are cited in this book. Again, an unbalanced approach to growth leads to investor skepticism about the future and low valuations.

Our multiyear growth study leads us to several questions managers should ask as they reflect on their own strategies:

- Where is our current business in its growth cycle (optimizing the core, adjacencies, redefinition)? Many managers, we find, are not sure.

- How many of our resources are focused on areas that have the potential to build market power and influence and drive for leadership economics in the core? How many are focused on inevitable follower positions?

- What *really* is the full potential of my core, and where does that potential reside?
  - Share gain in the core
  - Shift in the business mix to growing segments and channels
  - Pricing
  - New core products
  - Cost reduction
  - New customers or share gain in existing customers
  - Adjacencies involving new customers or new products

- Is there a repeatable formula driving my share gain, or success in adjacency expansion? What is it? Have I taken full advantage of the power of repeatability?

- What, realistically, is the "state of the core"? Where is it under threat? Where is it eroding? Where is it strengthening? How does the core need to change in the future? How will I do that?

- Are unconventional competitors making incursions at the fringe of our business? Does that signal the need to adapt the core faster? How?

Armed with this data, and ideas and examples like those in this book, managers should be constantly vigilant in tracking the three most dangerous long-term patterns we have identified. The first is premature abandonment of the core in favor of far-flung new adjacencies. Signs of erosion in the core or diffusion across too many initiatives will reveal this problem. The second is excessive mining of a core business, failing to put in place large enough new growth vehicles soon enough. If more earnings growth is consistently coming from these operating and cost-based initiatives than from core growth, there is clear danger. The third pattern is failure to anticipate the need for core redefinition. By the time competitors with new business models are taking your customers, you have probably waited too long to react.

Is It an Organizational Problem or a Strategy Problem?

A key issue for senior executives wrestling with growth problems or frustrations is determining whether the company's strategy is wrong or whether the organization is not able to execute it. Sometimes these problems can coexist and are difficult to separate. A strategy built for an organization that cannot execute it is not a good strategy, by definition. Conversely, a superb organization can shape and adapt even a mediocre strategy into a winner.

In high-growth markets, the most common organization-versus-strategy problem is inadequate management capacity for growth and rapid decision making combined with a lack of central direction, allowing many marginal and defocusing growth initiatives to sap resources. Jim Vincent, former CEO of Biogen, a classic "profit from the core" success story across the sweep of its history, has argued convincingly in interviews that this capacity issue is the number one CEO growth constraint, in his experience. The solution involves focusing more tightly around a strategy and, frequently, introducing management capabilities to deal with a larger, more complex, faster-moving company. The history of management in both the computer industry and Internet start-ups shows this pattern over and over.

In lower-growth markets, the most common problem is excessive mining of the core combined with a failure to see the emerging new landscape and possibilities. Often the historic management team has done a superb job of building and tending the core but along the way has acquired biases and habits that make it difficult to see the need for and commit serious resources to a strategic shift. The solution often requires the injection of new management talent along with a strategic redirection.

Ten Key Questions for Management

We close with ten questions that we believe management teams should periodically ask themselves about their companies and should include at the start of every review of their basic growth strategy. Certainly, companies find themselves in an almost infinite variety of strategic situations. However, we believe that these questions have universal applicability for companies, ranging from dominant product businesses trying to decide how to deal with the Internet to distribution companies wrestling with the sudden unbundling of their value chain to online companies trying to look beyond the "profitless prosperity" dream of today toward the requirements for sustained, profitable growth.

1. What is the most tightly defined profitable core of our business, and is it gaining or losing strength?

2. What defines the boundaries of the business that we are competing for, and where are those boundaries going to shift in the future?

3. Are there new competitors currently at the fringe of our business that pose potential longer-term threats to the core?

4. Are we certain that we are achieving the full strategic and operating potential of our core business, the "hidden value" of the core?

5. What is the full set of potential adjacencies to our core business and possible adjacency moves (single or multiple

moves)? Are we looking at these in a planned, logical sequence or piecemeal?

6. What is our point of view on the future of the industry? As a team, do we have consensus? How is this point of view shaping our adjacency strategy and point of arrival?

7. Should major new growth initiatives be pursued inside, next to, or outside the core? How should we decide?

8. Is industry turbulence changing the fundamental source of future competitive advantage? How? Through new models? New segments? New competitors? And what are we monitoring on a regular basis?

9. Are organizational enablers and inhibitors to growth in the right balance for the needed change?

10. What are the guiding strategic principles that should apply consistently to all of our major strategic and operating decisions?

Although military analogies to strategy are currently out of favor, we remain struck by the contemporary relevance of this observation from Sun-Tzu's *Art of War*: "The more opportunities that I seize, the more opportunities that multiply before me."[1] This phenomenon is at the heart of growth strategy and embodies the fundamental tension between protecting the core and driving into more and more adjacencies, propelled by greater and greater success. The Alexander problem described earlier will always be with us. However, we hope that the guiding principles and lessons learned from success and failure can help improve the odds for business managers battling in a world of greater uncertainty, more options, less time, bigger rewards and penalties, and higher complexity than ever before.

Notes

Preface

1. Chris Zook, *Unstoppable: Finding Hidden Assets to Renew the Core and Fuel Profitable Growth* (Boston: Harvard Business School Press, 2007).

Chapter 1: Desperately Seeking Growth

1. Mary Stuart, "A White Knight for Bausch & Lomb," *In Vivo*, June 2007.

2. Thomas A. Stewart and Julia Kirby, "The Institutional Yes: An Interview with Jeff Bezos," *Harvard Business Review*, October 2008.

3. Charles Goldsmith, "A Dying Lens Maker Zooms Back," *Wall Street Journal*, 23 March 2000.

4. John Micklethwait and Adrian Wooldridge, "Oxford Dons vs. Management Gurus," *Wall Street Journal*, 8 November 1996.

5. In a sense, our definition is a long-term version of the definitions used by G. Bennett Stewart III in *The Quest for Value* (New York: HarperBusiness, 1991), which drive off of economic returns relative to the long-term cost of capital.

6. Bernard Wysocki, Jr., "Corporate America Confronts the Meaning of a 'Core' Business," *Wall Street Journal*, 9 November 1999.

7. Clayton M. Christensen, *The Innovator's Dilemma: When New Technologies Cause Great Firms to Fail* (Boston: Harvard Business School Press, 1997).

8. Carl Shapiro and Hal R. Varian, *Information Rules: A Strategic Guide to the Network Economy* (Boston: Harvard Business School Press, 1999).

Chapter 2: The Profitable Core

1. Thomas J. Peters and Robert H. Waterman, *In Search of Excellence: Lessons from America's Best-Run Companies* (New York: HarperBusiness Essentials,

2004); C. K. Prahalad and Gary Hamel, "Core Competence of the Corporation," *Harvard Business Review*, May–June 1990; James C. Collins and Jerry I. Porras, *Built to Last: Successful Habits of Visionary Companies* (New York: HarperBusiness, 1994).

2. Mitt Romney, interview by Chris Zook, Boston, 12 June 1998.

3. David Sadtler, Andrew Campbell, and Richard Koch, *Break Up!* (Oxford: Capstone Publishing, 1997), 33.

4. Andrew Bary, "Why Catch a Knife?" *Barron's*, 6 October 1997, 17.

5. Steven Lipin and Nikhil Deogun, "Pepsi Announces Spinoff of Eateries, and Stock Soars," *Wall Street Journal*, 24 January 1997.

6. Ibid.

7. Ibid.

8. Constantinos C. Markides, *Diversification, Refocusing, and Economic Performance* (Cambridge, MA: MIT Press, 1995), 9.

9. Michael E. Porter, "From Competitive Advantage to Corporate Strategy," *Harvard Business Review*, May–June 1987.

10. Michael C. Mankins, David Harding, and Rolf-Magnus Weddigen, "How the Best Divest," *Harvard Business Review*, October 2008.

11. David Harding and Sam Rovit, with Katie Smith Milway and Catherine Lemire, *Mastering the Merger: Four Critical Decisions That Make or Break the Deal* (Boston: Harvard Business School Press, 2004).

12. Michael Dell, interview by Chris Zook, Dell headquarters, Austin, TX, March 26, 1999. See also Michael Dell with Catherine Fredman, *Direct from Dell: Strategies That Revolutionized an Industry* (New York: HarperBusiness, 1999).

13. Philip Evans and Thomas S. Wurster, *Blown to Bits: How the New Economics of Information Transforms Strategy* (Boston: Harvard Business School Press, 1999); and "Getting Real About Virtual Commerce," *Harvard Business Review*, November–December 1999. By far the best integrated and most original view on this topic is Carl Shapiro and Hal R. Varian, *Information Rules: A Strategic Guide to the Network Economy* (Boston: Harvard Business School Press, 1999). For additional readings on topics that bear on the increased blurring of business definition and the management challenges in the Internet economy, see Joan Magretta, ed., *Managing in the New Economy* (Boston: Harvard Business School Press, 1999).

Until the late 1970s, most business definition was put in terms of products and traditional market boundaries. In the 1980s, writers and theorists such as Derek Abell began looking more fundamentally at boundaries created by basic customer need (e.g., transportation versus railroad) and technology as potential ways to define a business. The next wave of thinking (Prahalad and Hamel) introduced the idea of the core competence as a source of ultimate competitive advantage in a core business and as a way of defining the boundaries of a business. For instance, recognizing ServiceMaster's expertise at managing large numbers of employees performing basic services leads to a clearer understanding of its business definition than looking just at cleaning services for businesses.

14. Bain & Company, "The Value of Online Customer Loyalty and How You Can Capture It," monograph, Bain & Company, Boston, 2000.

15. Fred Reichheld, *The Ultimate Question: Driving Good Profits And True Growth* (Boston: Harvard Business School Press, 2006).

16. Carl Everett, interview by Chris Zook, Austin, TX, February 1999.

17. Paul Larson, "Advanced Micro Devices, Inc.: How Did It Find Trouble?" 5 March 1999, www.fool.com, (accessed 15 November 1999).

18. For the best statement of this general point of view, see Michael Porter, "What Is Strategy?" *Harvard Business Review*, November–December 1996.

Chapter 3: The Alexander Problem

1. Allan Sloan, "80's Deals Showed American Express Could Use a Dose of Street Smarts," *Washington Post*, 16 March 1993.

2. Alex Pham, "Microsoft Targets America's Gamers," *Boston Globe*, 11 March 2000.

3. David Sheff, "Sony's Plan for World Recreation," *Wired*, November 1999, 3.

4. Gretchen Morgenson, "On the Acquisitions Road, Stay Alert to the Hazards," *New York Times*, 10 October 1999, sec. 3.

5. Ibid.

6. Chris Reidyo, "Gillette Sells Its Stationery Line," *Boston Globe*, 23 August 2000.

7. James C. Collins and Jerry I. Porras, *Built to Last: Successful Habits of Visionary Companies* (New York: HarperBusiness, 1994), 141.

8. Jay McCormack, "Amazing Grace: ServiceMaster Industries, Inc.," *Forbes*, 17 June 1985, 83.

9. Chris Zook, *Unstoppable: Finding Hidden Assets to Renew the Core and Fuel Profitable Growth* (Boston: Harvard Business School Press, 2007).

10. Ron Grover, *The Disney Touch: Disney, ABC & the Quest for the World's Greatest Media Empire* (Chicago: Irwin Professional Publishing), 3.

11. Bruce Orwall and Matthew Rose, "Disney Held Talks with Conde Nast, Hearst to Sell Fairchild Magazine Unit," *Wall Street Journal*, 16 August 1999.

12. Phil Buxton, "New Medicine," *Marketing Week*, 26 October 1999, 28.

13. Sydney Finkelstein and Shade H. Sanford, "Learning from Corporate Mistakes: The Rise and Fall of Iridium," *Organizational Dynamics* 29, no. 2 (2000): 138–148.

14. C. K. Prahalad and Gary Hamel, "Core Competence of the Corporation," *Harvard Business Review*, May–June 1990, 79.

15. Perhaps the best survey of this topic is provided by Carl Shapiro and Hal R. Varian in *Information Rules: A Strategic Guide to the Network Economy* (Boston: Harvard Business School Press, 1999).

16. We do not address this topic in this book; however, see Martha Amram and Nalin Kulatilaka, *Real Options: Managing Strategic Investment in an Uncertain World* (Boston: Harvard Business School Press, 1999).

17. John Keegan, *The Mask of Command* (New York: Viking–Elisabeth Sifton Books, 1987), 83–84.

18. Mitt Romney, interview by Chris Zook, Boston, 12 June 1998.

19. Orit Gadiesh and James L. Gilbert, "Profit Pools: A Fresh Look at Strategy," *Harvard Business Review*, May–June 1998, 141.

Chapter 4: The Redefinition Dilemma

1. Throughout this book, we have used analogies from biology. More than any other source, we have drawn our understanding, as well as this example, from Edward O. Wilson, *The Diversity of Life* (Cambridge, MA: Belknap Press of Harvard University Press, 1992).

2. In the future, sustained growth companies will be those that have been able to respond to today's turbulence in their industry and use it as a catalyst for change. A recent Bain survey of senior executives suggested that 91 percent of them believed that industry turbulence makes having a clear strategy more important than ever. More than 61 percent of them stated that they were worried about turbulence, and 73 percent said that they felt that their organizations suffered a false sense of security. (Darrell Rigby, "Winning in Turbulence," Bain & Company, Boston, 1999.) Those companies whose core businesses may need fundamental redefinition will face the difficult choice of transforming internally or developing a separate business into which skills and assets from the original core business are infused.

3. Arie de Geus, "The Living Company," *Harvard Business Review*, March–April 1997, 23.

4. "How to Live Long and Prosper," *Economist*, 10 May 1997.

5. de Geus, "The Living Company."

6. There is a massive body of literature about the remarkably poor record of results that came from the reengineering fad. See the following: John P. Kotter, "Leading Change: Why Transformational Efforts Fail," *Harvard Business Review*, March–April 1995; Fran Simons, "Transforming Change," *Australian Financial Review*, 26 March 1999; Constant D. Beugre, "Implementing Business Process Reengineering," *Journal of Applied Behavioral Science* 34, no. 3 (1998); Thomas

A. Stewart, "Reengineering: The Hot New Managing Tool," *Fortune*, 23 August 1993; and Brian Harrison, "How to Fail at Reengineering," *Directors & Boards* (Fall 1994).

7. Gary Jacobson and John Hillkirk, *Xerox: American Samurai* (New York: Collier Books, 1986).

8. Rajesh K. Chandy and Gerald J. Tellis, "Organizing for Radical Product Innovation: The Overlooked Role of Willingness to Cannibalize," *Journal of Marketing Research* (November 1998).

Chapter 5: Growing from the Core

1. Sun-Tzu, *The Art of War* (London: Oxford University Press, 1984).

Bibliography

Books

Abell, Derek. *Defining the Business: The Starting Point of Strategic Planning.* New York: Prentice-Hall, 1980.

Amram, Martha, and Nalin Kulatilaka. *Real Options: Managing Strategic Investment in an Uncertain World.* Boston: Harvard Business School Press, 1999.

Burrough, Bryan. *Barbarians at the Gate: The Fall of RJR Nabisco.* New York: HarperCollins, 1991.

Carroll, Glenn R., and Michael T. Hannon. *The Demography of Corporations and Industries.* Princeton, NJ: Princeton University Press, 2000.

Chandler, Alfred D., Jr. *Scale and Scope: The Dynamics of Industrial Capitalism.* Cambridge, MA: Belknap Press of Harvard University Press, 1990.

Chesbrough, Henry. *Open Innovation.* Boston: Harvard Business School Press, 2003.

Christensen, Clayton M. *The Innovator's Dilemma: When New Technologies Cause Great Firms to Fail.* Boston: Harvard Business School Press, 1997.

Cody, Thomas G. *Innovating for Health: The Story of Baxter International.* Deerfield, IL: Baxter International Inc., 1994.

Collins, Douglas. *America's Favorite Food: The Story of Campbell Soup Company.* New York: Harry N. Adams, 1994.

Collins, James C., and Jerry I. Porras. *Built to Last: Successful Habits of Visionary Companies.* New York: HarperBusiness, 1997.

Collins, Jim. *Good to Great.* New York: HarperBusiness, 2001.

Davies, S., et al. *The Dynamics of Market Leadership in the U.K. Manufacturing Industry 1979–1986.* London: Centre for Business Strategy, 1991.

Day, George S., and David J. Reibstein. *Wharton on Dynamic Competitive Strategy.* New York: John Wiley & Sons, 1997.

de Geus, Arie. *The Living Company*. Boston: Harvard Business School Press, 1997.

Dell, Michael, with Catherine Fredman. *Direct from Dell: Strategies That Revolutionized an Industry*. New York: HarperBusiness, 1999.

Evans, Philip, and Thomas S. Wurster. *Blown to Bits: How the New Economics of Information Transforms Strategy*. Boston: Harvard Business School Press, 1999.

Farkas, Charles M., Philippe De Backer, and Allen Sheppard. *Maximum Leadership: The World's Top Leaders Discuss How They Add Value to Companies*. London: Orion, 1995.

Goold, Michael, Andrew Campbell, and Marcus Alexander. *Corporate-Level Strategy: Creating Value in the Multibusiness Company*. New York: John Wiley & Sons, 1994.

Grove, Andrew S. *Only the Paranoid Survive: How to Exploit the Crisis Points That Challenge Every Company*. New York: Bantam Books, 1999.

Grover, Ron. *The Disney Touch: Disney, ABC & the Quest for the World's Greatest Media Empire*. Chicago: Irwin Professional Publishing, 1991.

Hamel, Gary. *Leading the Revolution*. Boston: Harvard Business School Press, 2000.

Hamel, Gary, and C. K. Prahalad. *Competing for the Future*. Boston: Harvard Business School Press, 1994.

Hannan, Michael T., and John Freeman. *Organizational Ecology*. Cambridge: Harvard University Press, 1989.

Harding, David, and Sam Rovit. *Mastering the Merger: Four Critical Decisions that Make or Break the Deal*. Boston: Harvard Business School Press, 2004.

Harvard Business Review on Strategies for Growth. Boston: Harvard Business School Press, 1998.

Imparato, Nicholas, and Oren Harari. *Jumping the Curve*. San Francisco: Jossey-Bass Publishers, 1994.

Jackson, Tim. *Inside Intel*. New York: Penguin Books, 1997.

Jacobson, Gary, and John Hillkirk. *Xerox: American Samurai*. New York: Collier Books, Macmillan Publishing, 1986.

Janus, Irving. *Groupthink*. Boston: Houghton Mifflin, 1982.

Jonash, Ronald S., and Tom Sommerlatte. *The Innovation Premium*. New York: Perseus Books, 1999.

Kaplan, Robert S., and David P. Norton. *The Balanced Scorecard: Translating Strategy into Action*. Boston: Harvard Business School Press, 1996.

Katz, Donald. *Just Do It*. Holbrook, MA: Adams Media Corp., 1997.

Keegan, John. *The Mask of Command*. New York: Viking–Elisabeth Sifton Books, 1987.

Keynes, John Maynard. *A Treatise on Probability*. London: Macmillan, 1921.

Kim, W. Chan, and Renée Mauborgne. *Blue Ocean Strategy*. Boston: Harvard Business School Press, 2005.

Leonard-Barton, Dorothy. *Wellsprings of Knowledge*. Cambridge: Harvard Business School Press, 1995.

Lorsch, Jay W., and Thomas J. Tierney. *Aligning the Stars: How to Succeed When Professionals Drive Results*. Boston: Harvard Business School Press, 2002.

Magretta, Joan, ed. *Managing in the New Economy*. Boston: Harvard Business School Press, 1999.

Markides, Constantinos C. *Diversification, Refocusing, and Economic Performance*. Cambridge, MA: MIT Press, 1995.

Markides, Constantinos C., and Paul A. Geroski. *Fast Second: How Smart Companies Bypass Radical Innovation to Enter and Dominate New Markets*. San Francisco: Jossey-Bass, 2004.

Mintzberg, Henry. *The Rise and Fall of Strategic Planning*. New York: Prentice-Hall, 1994.

Montgomery, Cynthia A., and Michael E. Porter, eds. *Strategy: Seeking and Securing Competitive Advantage*. Boston: Harvard Business School Press, 1991.

Moore, Geoffrey A. *Inside the Tornado: Marketing Strategies from Silicon Valley's Cutting Edge*. New York: HarperBusiness, 1995.

———. *Crossing the Chasm: Marketing and Selling High-Tech Products to Mainstream Consumers*. New York: HarperBusiness, 1999.

Olson, Matthew S., and Derek van Bever. *Stall Points: Most Companies Stop Growing—Yours Doesn't Have To*. New Haven, CT: Yale University Press, 2008.

Peters, Thomas J., and Robert H. Waterman, Jr. *In Search of Excellence: Lessons from America's Best-Run Companies*. New York: Harper & Row Publishers, 1982.

Porter, Michael E. *Competitive Strategy*. New York: Free Press, 1980.

———. *Competitive Advantage*. New York: Free Press, 1985.

Pottruck, David S., and Terry Pearce. *Clicks and Mortar: Passion-Driven Growth in an Internet-Driven World*. San Francisco: Jossey-Bass Publishers, 2000.

Quinn, James Brian, Jordan J. Baruch, and Karen Anne Zien. *Innovation Explosion: Using Intellect and Software to Revolutionize Growth Strategies*. New York: Free Press, 1997.

Ravenscroft, David J., Robert D. Buzzell, and Bradley T. Gale. *The PIMS Principles: Linking Strategy to Performance*. New York: Free Press, 1987.

Read, Donald. *The Power of News: The History of Reuters*, 2d ed. Oxford: Oxford University Press, 1999.

Reichheld, Frederick F. *The Loyalty Effect: The Hidden Force Behind Growth, Profits, and Lasting Value*. Boston: Harvard Business School Press, 1996.

————. *Loyalty Rules!* Boston: Harvard Business School Press, 2001.

————. *The Ultimate Question: Driving Good Profits and True Growth*. Boston: Harvard Business School Press, 2006.

Rothschild, Michael. *Bionomics: Economy as Ecosystem*. New York: Henry Holt, 1990.

Rumelt, Richard P., Dan E. Schendel, and David J. Teece, eds. *Fundamental Issues in Strategy: A Research Agenda*. Boston: Harvard Business School Press, 1994.

Sadtler, David, Andrew Campbell, and Richard Koch. *Break Up!* Oxford: Capstone Publishing, 1997.

Schrage, Michael. *Serious Play: How the World's Best Companies Simulate to Innovate*. Cambridge: Harvard Business School Press, 2000.

Schumpeter, Joseph. *Capitalism, Socialism and Democracy*. New York: Harper, 1942.

Shapiro, Carl, and Hal R. Varian. *Information Rules: A Strategic Guide to the Network Economy*. Boston: Harvard Business School Press, 1999.

Shiller, Robert. *Irrational Exuberance*. Princeton: Princeton University Press, 2000.

Sirower, Mark L. *The Synergy Trap: How Companies Lose the Acquisition Game*. New York: Free Press, 1997.

Slater, Robert. *Jack Welch and the GE Way*. New York: McGraw-Hill, 1999.

Slywotzky, Adrian J. *Value Migration: How to Think Several Moves Ahead of the Competition*. Boston: Harvard Business School Press, 1995.

Slywotsky, Adrian, and Richard Wise. *How to Grow When Markets Don't*. New York: Warner Business Books, 2003.

Stalk, George Jr., and Thomas M. Hout. *Competing Against Time: How Time-Based Competition Is Reshaping Global Markets*. New York: Free Press, 1990.

Stemberg, Thomas S. *Staples for Success*. Santa Monica, CA: Knowledge Exchange, 1996.

Stewart, G. Bennett III. *The Quest for Value*. New York: Stern/Stewart, 1993.

Sun-Tzu. *The Art of War*. London: Oxford University Press, 1984.

Swisher, Kara. *aol.com*. New York: Random House, 1998.

Tichy, Noel M., and Stratford Sherman. *Control Your Destiny or Someone Else Will*. London: HarperCollins, 1995.

Utterback, James M. *Mastering the Dynamics of Innovation*. Boston: Harvard Business School Press, 1994.

Viguerie, Patrick, Sven Smit, and Mehrdad Baghai. *The Granularity of Growth: How to Identify the Sources of Growth and Drive Enduring Company Performance*. Hoboken, NJ: John Wiley & Sons, Inc., 2008.

Wilson, Edward O. *The Diversity of Life*. Cambridge, MA: Harvard University Press, 1992.

Zook, Chris. *Beyond the Core: Expand Your Market Without Abandoning Your Roots*. Boston: Harvard Business School Press, 2004.

Zook, Chris. *Unstoppable: Finding Hidden Assets To Renew the Core and Fuel Profitable Growth*. Boston: Harvard Business School Press, 2007.

Articles

Abell, Derek F. "Competing Today While Preparing for Tomorrow." *Sloan Management Review*, Spring 1999.

Anslinger, and Thomas E. Copeland. "Growth Through Acquisitions: A Fresh Look." *Harvard Business Review*, January–February 1996.

Avila, Joe, Nat Mass, and Mark Turchan. "Keys to Profitable Growth." *The McKinsey Quarterly*, no. 1 (1996).

Baden-Fuller, Charles and Henk W. Volberda. "Strategic Renewal: How Large Complex Organizations Prepare for the Future." *International Studies of Management & Organization*, 22 June 1997.

Bain & Company. "The Value of Online Customer Loyalty and How You Can Capture It." Monograph, Bain & Company, Boston, 2000.

Bary, Andrew. "Why Catch a Knife?" *Barron's*, 6 October 1997.

Bechek, Bob, and Chris Zook. "The Jenga Phenomenon." White paper, Bain & Company, Boston, 1999.

Beinhocker, Eric D. "Robust Adaptive Strategies." *Sloan Management Review*, Spring 1999.

Berger, Philip, and Eli Ofek. "Diversification's Effect on Firm Value." *Journal of Financial Economics*, 37 (1995).

Beugre, Constant D. "Implementing Business Process Reengineering." *Journal of Applied Behavioral Science*, 34, no. 3 (1998).

Bower, Joseph L., and Clayton M. Christensen. "Disruptive Technologies: Catching the Wave." *Harvard Business Review*, January–February 1995.

Brian, W. Arthur. "Increasing Returns and the New World of Business." *Harvard Business Review*, July–August 1996.

Brooks, Rick. "UPS's New eVentures Unit Plans to Expand Logistics Business." *Wall Street Journal*, 7 February 2000.

Buxton, Phil. "New Medicine." *Marketing Week*, 26 October 1999.

Campbell, Andrew, Michael Goold, and Marcus Alexander. "Corporate Strategy: The Quest for Parenting Advantage." *Harvard Business Review*, March–April 1995.

Caves, Richard E., B. T. Gale, and Michael E. Porter. "Interfirm Profitability Differences." *Quarterly Journal of Economics*, November 1977.

Chandy, Rajesh K., and Gerald J. Tellis. "Organizing for Radical Product Innovation: The Overlooked Role of Willingness to Cannibalize." *Journal of Marketing Research*, November 1998.

Charan, Ram, and Geoffrey Colvin. "Why CEOs Fail." *Fortune*, 21 June 1999.

Collis, David J., and Cynthia A. Montgomery. "Competing on Resources: Strategy in the 1990s." *Harvard Business Review*, July–August 1995.

Comment, Robert, and Gregg A. Jarrell. "Corporate Focus and Stock Returns." *Journal of Financial Economics*, 37 (1995).

Corporate Strategy Board. "Stall Points: Barriers to Growth for the Large Corporate Enterprise." Monograph, The Advisory Board Company, Washington, DC, 1997.

Courtney, Hugh, Jane Kirkland, and Patrick Viguerie. "Strategy Under Uncertainty." *Harvard Business Review*, November–December 1997.

D'Aveni, Richard A. "Strategic Supremacy Through Disruption and Dominance." *Sloan Management Review*, Spring 1999.

Day, George S. "Creating a Market Driven Organization." *Sloan Management Review*, Fall 1999.

de Geus, Arie. "The Living Company." *Harvard Business Review*, March–April 1997.

DeLlosa, Patty. "How Coke Is Kicking Pepsi's Can." *Fortune*, 28 October 1996.

Dolan, Kerry A. "Judo Attack." *Forbes*, 9 March 1998.

Drucker, Peter F. "The Information Executives Truly Need." *Harvard Business Review*, January–February 1995.

Eisenhardt, Kathleen M., and Shona L. Brown. "The Art of Continuous Change: Linking Complexity Theory and Time-Paced Evolution in Relentlessly Shifting Organizations." *Administrative Science Quarterly*, March 1997.

———. "Time Pacing: Competing in Markets That Won't Stand Still." *Harvard Business Review*, March–April 1998.

———. "Patching: Restitching Business Portfolios in Dynamic Markets." *Harvard Business Review*, May–June 1999.

Evans, Philip B. and Thomas S. Wurster. "Strategy and the New Economics of Information." *Harvard Business Review*, September–October 1997.

———. "Getting Real About Virtual Commerce." *Harvard Business Review*, November–December 1999.

Farkas, Charles M., and Bob Bechek. "Rebuilding Banking Piecemeal, On Web." *American Banker*, 28 May 1999.

Farkas, Charles M., and Suzy Wetlaufer. "The Ways Chief Executive Officers Lead." *Harvard Business Review*, May–June 1996.

"Fear of the Unknown." *Economist*, 4 December 1999.

Finkelstein, Sydney, and Shade H. Sanford. "Learning from Corporate Mistakes: The Rise and Fall of Iridium." *Organizational Dynamics*, November 2000, 138–148.

Finnie, William C. "A Four-Cycle Approach to Strategy Development and Implementation." *Strategy & Leadership*, January–February 1997.

Fisher, Anne B. "Making Change Stick." *Fortune*, 17 April 1995.

"Fortune 500." *Fortune*, 26 April 1999.

Gadiesh, Orit, and James L. Gilbert. "How to Map Your Industry's Profit Pool." *Harvard Business Review*, May–June 1998.

———. "Profit Pools: A Fresh Look at Strategy." *Harvard Business Review*, May–June 1998.

Geroski, Paul A. "Early Warning of New Rivals." *Sloan Management Review*, Spring 1999.

Goldsmith, Charles. "A Dying Lens Maker Zooms Back." *Wall Street Journal*, 23 March 2000.

Goold, Michael and Andrew Campbell. "Many Best Ways to Make Strategy." *Harvard Business Review*, November–December 1987.

———. "Desperately Seeking Synergy." *Harvard Business Review*, September–October 1998.

Hamel, Gary. "Strategy as Revolution." *Harvard Business Review*, July–August 1996.

———. "Killer Strategies That Make Shareholders Rich." *Fortune*, 23 June 1997.

———. "Opinion: Strategy Innovation and the Quest for Value." *Sloan Management Review*, Winter 1998.

Hamel, Gary, and C. K. Prahalad. "Competing for the Future." *Harvard Business Review*, July–August 1994.

Hannan, Michael T., and John Freeman. "Structural Inertia and Organizational Change." *American Sociological Review*, April 1984.

Harrison, Brian. "How to Fail at Reengineering." *Directors & Boards*, Fall 1994.

Hart, Stuart L., and Mark B. Milstein. "Global Sustainability and the Creative Destruction of Industries." *Sloan Management Review*, Fall 1999.

Henderson, Bruce D. "The Origins of Strategy." *Harvard Business Review*, November–December 1989.

Holstein, William J. "The Dot Com within Ford." *U.S. News & World Report*, 7 February 2000.

"How to Live Long and Prosper." *Economist*, 10 May 1997.

Kaplan, Robert S., and David P. Norton. "The Balanced Scorecard: Measures That Drive Performance." *Harvard Business Review*, January–February 1992.

Kim, W. Chan, and Renee Mauborgne. "Value Innovation: The Strategic Logic of High Growth." *Harvard Business Review*, January–February 1997.

———. "When Competitive Advantage Is Neither." *Wall Street Journal*, Manager's Journal, 21 April 1997.

———. "Strategy, Value Innovation and the Knowledge Economy." *Sloan Management Review*, Spring 1999.

Knight, Charles F. "Emerson Electric: Consistent Profits, Consistently." *Harvard Business Review*, January–February 1992.

Kotter, John P. "Leading Change: Why Transformational Efforts Fail." *Harvard Business Review*, March–April 1995.

Larson, Paul. "Advanced Micro Devices, Inc.: How Did It Find Trouble?" 5 March 1999. www.fool.com (accessed November 15, 1999).

Leonard, Russell L., Jr. "Reengineering: The Missing Links." *Human Resource Planning*, 19, no. 4 (1996).

Leonard-Barton, Dorothy. "Core Capabilities and Core Rigidities: A Paradox in Managing New Product Development." *Strategic Management Journal*, 13 (1992).

Lipin, Steven, and Nikhil Deogun. "Pepsi Announces Spinoff of Eateries, and Stock Soars." *Wall Street Journal*, 24 January 1997.

———. "Pepsi Shares Leap on Report of Spinoff of Restaurant Unit." *Wall Street Journal Europe*, 24 January 1997.

Mankins, Michael C., David Harding, and Rolf-Magnus Weddigen, "How the Best Divest." *Harvard Business Review*, October 2008.

Markides, Constantinos C. "Strategic Innovation." *Sloan Management Review*, Spring 1997.

———. "To Diversify or Not To Diversify." *Harvard Business Review*, November–December 1997.

———. "Strategic Innovation in Established Companies." *Sloan Management Review*, Spring 1998.

———. "A Dynamic View of Strategy." *Sloan Management Review*, Spring 1999.

Marshall, Cheri T., and Robert D. Buzzell. "PIMS and the FTC Line-Of-Business Data: A Comparison." *Strategic Management Journal*, 11 (1990).

McCormack, Jay. "Amazing Grace: ServiceMaster Industries, Inc." *Forbes*, 17 June 1985.

Micklethwait, John, and Adrian Wooldridge. "Oxford Dons vs. Management Gurus." *Wall Street Journal*, 8 November 1996.

Mintzberg, Henry, and Joseph Lampel. "Reflecting on the Strategy Process." *Sloan Management Review*, Spring 1999.

Monk, Nina. "Title Fight." *Fortune*, 21 June 1999.

Morgenson, Gretchen. "On the Acquisitions Road, Stay Alert to the Hazards." *New York Times*, 10 October 1999.

O'Reilly, Brian. "They've Got Mail: UPS vs. FedEx." *Fortune*, 7 February 2000.

Orwall, Bruce, and Matthew Rose. "Disney Held Talks with Conde Nast, Hearst to Sell Fairchild Magazine Unit." *Wall Street Journal*, 16 August 1999.

Pham, Alex. "Microsoft Targets America's Gamers." *Boston Globe*, 11 March 2000.

Porter, Michael E. "From Competitive Advantage to Corporate Strategy." *Harvard Business Review*, May–June 1987.

———. "What Is Strategy?" *Harvard Business Review*, November–December 1996.

Prahalad, C. K., and Gary Hamel. "Core Competence of the Corporation." *Harvard Business Review*, May–June 1990.

Prahalad, C. K., and Venkatram Ramaswamy. "Co-opting Customer Competence." *Harvard Business Review*, January–February 2000.

Quinn, Sue. "Nokia Share Price Stays Upwardly Mobile." *Sun Herald*, 23 January 2000.

Raynovich, R. Scott. "Intel's Got Internet Inside." *Redherring.com*, 11 August 1999.

Reidyo, Chris. "Gillette Sells Its Stationery Line." *Boston Globe*, 23 August 2000.

Reingold, Jennifer. "Doesn't Work, Doesn't Matter." *BusinessWeek*, 31 May 1999.

Rigby, Darrell K. "What's Today's Special At the Consultants' Café?" *Fortune*, 7 September 1998.

———. "Management Tools & Techniques 1999: An Executive's Guide." Bain & Company, Boston, 1999.

———. "Winning in Turbulence: Strategies for Success in Tumultuous Times." Bain & Company, Boston, 1999.

Rigby Darrell, and Chris Zook. "Open-Market Innovation." *Harvard Business Review*, October 2002, 80–89.

Rumelt, Richard P. "Diversification Strategy and Profitability." *Strategic Management Review*, 3 (1982).

———. "How Much Does Industry Matter?" *Strategic Management Review*, 12 (1991).

Schmalensee, Richard. "Do Markets Differ Much?" *American Economic Review*, June 1985.

"Shareholder Scoreboard." *Wall Street Journal*, 24 February 2000.

Sheff, David. "Sony's Plan for World Recreation." *Wired*, November 1999.

Silberman, Steve. "Just Say Nokia." *Wired*, September 1999.

Simison, Robert L., Fara Warner, and Gregory L. White. "Big Three Car Makers Plan Net Exchange—GM, Ford, DaimlerChrysler to Create a Single Firm to Supply Auto Parts." *Wall Street Journal*, 28 February 2000.

Simons, Fran. "Transforming Change." *Australian Financial Review*, 26 March 1999.

Sirower, Mark. "What Acquiring Minds Need to Know." *Wall Street Journal*, 22 February 1999.

Sloan, Allan. "80's Deals Showed American Express Could Use a Dose of Street Smarts." *Washington Post*, 16 March 1993.

Sohr, Steve. "Again, It's Microsoft vs. the World." *New York Times*, 13 February 2000.

"Spinning It Out at Thermo Electron," *Economist*, 12 April 1997.

Stalk, George Jr., David K. Pecaut, and Benjamin Burnett. "Breaking Compromises, Breakaway Growth." *Harvard Business Review*, September–October 1996.

Stewart, Thomas A. "Reengineering: The Hot New Managing Tool." *Fortune*, 23 August 1993.

Stewart, Thomas A., and Julia Kirby. "The Institutional Yes: An Interview with Jeff Bezos." *Harvard Business Review*, October 2007.

Stuart, Mary. "A White Knight for Bausch & Lomb." *In Vivo*, June 2007.

Teece, David J., Gary Pisano, and Amy Shuen. "Dynamic Capabilities and Strategic Management." *Strategic Management Journal*, 18 (1997).

Useem, Jerry. "Internet Defense Strategy: Cannibalize Yourself." *Fortune*, 6 September 1999.

Vishwanath, Vijay, and Jonathan Mark. "Your Brand's Best Strategy." *Harvard Business Review*, May–June 1997.

Wensley, Robin. "Explaining Success: The Rule of Ten Percent and the Example of Market Share." *Business Strategy Review*, 8, No.1 (1997).

WorldScope database provided by Disclosure First Contact. One of the most comprehensive data sources on public companies worldwide, containing financial information on more than 8,800 companies.

Wysocki, Bernard Jr. "Corporate America Confronts the Meaning of a 'Core Business.'" *Wall Street Journal*, 9 November 1999.

Yoffie, David B., and Michael A. Cusumano. "Judo Strategy: The Competitive Dynamics of Internet Time." *Harvard Business Review*, January–February 1999.

Zook, Chris. "Finding Your Next Core Business." *Harvard Business Review*, April 2007.

Zook, Chris, and James Allen. "Growth Outside the Core." *Harvard Business Review*, December 2003.

Index

About the Authors

CHRIS ZOOK is a director of Bain & Company, a global business strategy consulting firm, and co-head of Bain's Global Strategy practice. His client work has concentrated on how companies find their next wave of profitable growth, and he is the author of an extensive series of articles and books on that topic. He is a frequent speaker at global forums, such as the World Economic Forum at Davos, and was named by *The Times* of London as one of the fifty most influential global business thinkers. Zook currently splits his time between homes in Boston and Amsterdam.

JAMES ALLEN is a senior partner of Bain & Company and co-head of Bain's Global Strategy practice. He serves on Bain's board of directors and has served on its Management Committee and Nominating Committee. He founded Bain's Customer Strategy practice and has given numerous speeches on "The Consumer of 2020." He is also a frequent speaker at the World Economic Forum in Davos. With more than twenty years of consulting experience, Allen has worked extensively for multinationals in consumer products, oil and gas, technology, telecommunications, health care and other industries. Allen has advised clients on developing global growth strategies, emerging-market entry strategies, turnaround strategies and strategies for sustained innovation, and he has written about these and other topics for leading business publications, including *Harvard Business Review*.